129 More
SEMINAR
SPEAKING
SUCCESS
Tips

David R. Portney

KALLISTI PUBLISHING
WILKES-BARRE, PA

Kallisti Publishing, Inc.
332 Center Street
Wilkes-Barre, PA 18702
Phone (877) 444-6188 • Fax (419) 781-1907
www.kallistipublishing.com

Kallisti Publishing, Inc. titles may be purchased for business or promotional use or for special sales. Please contact Kallisti Publishing for more information.

Kallisti Publishing, Inc. and its logo are trademarks of Kallisti Publishing, Inc.

10 9 8 7 6 5 4 3 2 1

Library of Congress Control Number: 2008928633
ISBN 0-9678514-8-3
ISBN-13 978-0-9678514-8-8

DESIGNED & PRINTED IN THE UNITED STATES OF AMERICA

Table of Contents

Dedicated to people everywhere wishing to maximize their income and success through speaking and seminars...

Why & How You Should Read This Book

Some time ago I coined the term "seminar speaking success" as a simple yet broad way of talking about doing public speaking, seminars, workshops, client appreciation events —any kind of group event. If there are people gathered and you or someone else is speaking to that group, then that falls under the category of my term "seminar speaking".

Why do I add the word "success" to the end of that phrase? It's because the reality is that public speaking, seminars, and group events of all kinds are proving themselves to be one of the very few remaining viable and cost-effective ways to promote your business, product, service, cause, or issue.

In short, if you want to get your message in front of people inexpensively and effectively, your choices are shrinking quickly.

For example, even as I write these words, newspaper and magazine subscriptions are falling. I've personally interviewed a number of sales people working for various print publications, and while they initially try to paint a rosy picture about the state of their industry, inevitably they quietly confide "off the record" that fewer and fewer people are spending money on advertising with them. And it's not hard to understand why: as subscriptions fall and readership dwindles, advertisers in those publications see the results of their advertising efforts also dwindling. As most publications rely more on advertising dollars than subscriptions to stay in business, a vicious downward spiral ensues.

But it's not just a lack of subscribers that accounts for the declining effectiveness of advertising—people are increasingly jaded by commercial advertising and marketing. It's almost as if people are becoming immune to it. We're all bombarded with advertising and marketing messages seemingly from the moment we wake up to the moment we go to sleep. I'm sure that if marketing companies could figure out a way to advertise in our dreams, they'd do that in a New York minute. And in the meantime people are recording TV shows and zipping past commercials using DVRs and other digital recording technology and services. Advertisers are desperately scrambling to figure out how to get marketing messages to even be seen. More and more they're trying to weave their product or service into the actual scripts of movies and TV shows so that people have to see their "commercial". And as the Internet moves to a TV screen near you, traditional commercial advertisers will go the way of the dodo bird.

And it's not just businesses that suffer as consumers become pickier, have more choices, and develop immunity and allergic reactions to commercials and advertising. Because consumers feel besieged or even under attack by advertisers, any kind of request or demand for their attention or interest is eyed with suspicion and skepticism. That means that even reputable charity organizations, for example, have to work that much harder to capture the awareness and concern of modern consumers and citizens.

In other words, if you want to get your message out, you've got an uphill struggle. And that goes for any kind of message from any kind of organization—business, charity, political, community, or otherwise.

Let's cut through to the bottom line: if you want to reach people these days, those people want to make their own choice about hearing from you. You could call it "opt-in" marketing in the sense that people no longer will tolerate you "pushing" your message in front of them. If they're interested, they want to "pull your message in" by their doing, and not by your doing.

Smart marketers and advertisers have already realized this fact and have adjusted their approach accordingly. Some call it "relationship marketing". Relationship marketing means that instead of you pushing out your marketing message, you pull people in by offering them information they find interesting and appealing. But that doesn't mean you then turn around and clobber them with advertising as soon as you get their attention; it means you continue to give them useful information they need or desire, and you therefore build trust between you and them.

Then, by their choice, they may decide to look further into what you have to offer—but notice that this is by their choice, and it's their decision based on feeling comfortable with you and not because you hammered them with advertising.

As you give people useful, needed, desirable information, you establish trust, you create a comfort zone, and you build a relationship. Then when they need your product or service, you're naturally the first place they look because to them you're already the trusted source.

Obviously, it's the Internet that's primarily responsible for the consumers' shift away from push-marketing. People don't go to the Internet looking for advertising, commercials, and sales pitches. They go to the Internet looking for information they want and need. That's why at my websites —such as *PublicSpeakingWizard.com*, *SeminarAcademy. com*, *GreatPublicSpeakingTraining.com*, or *BestPublicSpeakingTraining.com*—I don't push products and services into people's faces. Instead, I have dozens of valuable free articles people can read. I even have a free subscription service visitors can opt-in for, delivering useful information to them weekly via email, and people can subscribe as long as they want and opt-out anytime they want, all by their choice.

But this shift in consumer attitude carries over to offline marketing as well. For example, people don't visit a car dealership to hear sales pitches, but rather to obtain information they don't already have so that then can then make better-informed buying decisions. The smart car dealers and auto sales people recognize this and look to make people comfortable instead of trying to force them into a buying decision they may regret later.

The reality is that people are just plain sick and tired of pushy sales people and transparent manipulative sales pitches.

By now it should be obvious to you what all this has to do with "seminar speaking success". **Public speaking and seminars remain as the perfect marketing and advertising solution to promote any business, service, product, charity, issue, or cause.**

First, public speaking and seminars do not push a message onto anyone that does not want to hear it. If someone's not interested in your message or topic, they're not going to show up to your speaking engagement or seminar in the first place. And even if they wind up there somehow "by accident" and don't want to be there, they can easily just get up and leave. That means seminars and public speaking are not "push" advertising or marketing because people are free to choose to attend or not attend according to their desire.

Second, public speaking and seminars allow you to provide valuable information people want and need, and at the same time gives you the perfect opportunity to build a relationship with people. In fact, public speaking and seminars are *the perfect way* to build relationships with people. Why? Because there you are up in front of the room giving them useful information—you're the expert on the topic. As you, the expert, are up there speaking, people look at your face and they listen to your voice and they get a "feel" for you and whether they like you, trust you, and believe you.

And that liking, that trust, that believing is the key because people want to do business with people they like, believe, and trust. Do you want to spend your hard-earned money with people you don't like? Or don't believe? Or don't trust? Of course not!

Hence, this book you're reading right now. And just in case you haven't noticed, the title of this book is *129 More Seminar Speaking Success Tips* because this is the follow up to my previous book *129 Seminar Speaking Success Tips*. Taken together, these two books comprise 258 hard-hitting tips and techniques you can use right away to build relationships with prospects and potential customers and clients using the most powerful method remaining to date: public speaking and seminars.

Just like my previous book *129 Seminar Speaking Success Tips*, you can think of this book like diving into a box of chocolates—you never know what you're going to get; that means you could simply open this book up to any page and be surprised and delighted by what you find. Of course, you could just read the book cover-to-cover if that's your desire. Another of many possibilities is that you could pick just one tip per day and incorporate and integrate just that one tip—which means that in just over a four-month period you'd have assimilated 129 valuable tips into your repertoire and abilities.

Of course, this is your book, so I advise you to bookmark pages, highlight sentences, and make notes in the margins as this book will not only give you great information, but also great inspiration. As you read the tips in this book it will spark your creativity and ingenuity. Write down your ideas as they come to you while you read this book because those ideas will prove to be as good as gold for you.

Remember the potato chip company that used to advertise with the slogan "Bet you can't eat just one!"? Well, I consider *129 More Seminar Speaking Success Tips* to be like a bag of potato chips, because when you read one tip, you'll want to read another!

Before you dive into the book, consider this: most career professionals, business owners, and entrepreneurs will never, ever make the minimal effort it takes to conquer stage fright and fear of public speaking, master expert presentation skills, and go on to do seminars and public speaking. That leaves you way ahead of the pack and far out in front of your competition!

Finally, feel free to browse my websites—*PublicSpeakingWizard.com, GreatPublicSpeakingTraining.com, SeminarAcademy.com*, and *BestPublicSpeakingTraining.com*—for even more tips, ideas, articles and my latest resources. Be sure to write or email me with your ideas, your thoughts, your feedback, and what you'd like to see more of from me. And send me your success stories too and I'll proudly publish them in my newsletter and on my website—that's great public kudos and recognition (and exposure!) for you, and serves as great inspiration for others to aspire to seminar speaking success as well.

Here's to your Seminar Speaking Success!

David R. Portney
December, 2008

129 More

SEMINAR SPEAKING SUCCESS

Tips

Let Your Light Shine Bright!

Passion captivates people. When others see someone feeling intensely about something, that gets noticed and in a big way—even if they don't agree, they still notice and remember the intensity of passion expressed.

Are you expressing passion in your seminar talk? The power of passion is something you should definitely use to your advantage.

Why do you do what you do? What's your purpose, your mission? What drives you? Share that with your group. It doesn't matter whether you're a real estate broker, insurance agent, chiropractor, plumber, or financial advisor, key into your purpose, your mission—your drive—and share that with others. Tell your group about it. People respond to those who are passionate. People are moved my passion. People are influenced by passion. Passion is contagious.

Tap into your passion by tapping into your sense of purpose and mission, then share your passion and let your light shine bright!

Like Magic!

Here's something you're going to notice after you've been doing seminar speaking for a while: *Time flies.* Your problems disappear. Being on stage is like a drug. Over the years, I've had seminars or workshops booked, but I was sick. I felt miserable. I dragged myself into the seminar room and set up. People gathered and before I knew it, it was "show time." I got up to speak and conduct the seminar. Then, it wasn't until after the seminar was over and I packed up to leave that I realized I was still sick. *I had forgotten I was sick while I was giving my talk!*

There is magic that happens that I can't attribute to just an adrenaline rush. I've been doing seminar speaking for so long now, it takes a lot to get my adrenaline pumping. Even speaking in front of hundreds of people is an ordinary affair, like putting on socks, something I've done a million times. So I don't think it's adrenaline that causes all your problems to go away once you hit the stage.

This is something that will happen to you, too. There is something magical about the exchange between you and your audience. Feel free to email me and share your experiences.

Sight, Smell, Hearing, Taste, and Touch

Are you appealing to people's full range of senses in your seminar speaking? One way to instantly become a better, and certainly more compelling seminar speaker is to be sure to address the full range of senses.

As you know, we all have five senses. The most important ones to utilize in your seminar speaking is the sense of sight, sound, and feeling. It's pretty unlikely that smell and taste are going to come into play unless your seminar involves perfumery products or food service, but it is nevertheless possible to include those as well. Speaking to people's senses creates a deeper involvement in what you're saying, and creates a more memorable experience. Paint pictures with your words. Describe things in ways that make people picture what you're saying. Use words to evoke familiar sounds, like music or other common sounds. Touch on their sense of feeling by using words that evoke texture, temperature, and other every day feeling experiences.

Review your talk with an eye to how you can use the power of words to evoke people's senses more fully—that creates a deeper, richer experience on the part of your audience.

Data, Facts, Statistics

Here's a sure-fire technique you can use anytime you could use a little boost in your expertise and want to enhance your credibility. Have right at your fingertips a mass of data, facts, and statistics. Be sure to have the sources as well, including specific names of persons and/or organizations that originated the data and facts.

When you start quoting a bunch of factual data and citing the sources, that rubs off on you. You look like you've really done a lot of research (and maybe you have!) and at the same time, you bask in the glow of all that work that was done by others.

Other peoples' expertise and hard work can actually help you to shine in your seminar speaking.

Face Your Fear!

Feel the fear, but do it anyway!

Maybe that sounds like "tough love", but it's just good advice. Naturally, I suggest you use the many techniques I teach you here and in my workshops to conquer stage fright and fear of public speaking. And, sometimes, it makes sense to take a leap of faith and just do what you're afraid to do.

If you wind up in a situation where you have the opportunity to give a talk and you're not sure you're 100% comfortable, *just do the talk anyway*. You know, sometimes acting in the face of fear can be a very empowering experience. Just ask someone who goes skydiving for the very first time. But unlike skydiving, you won't risk plummeting to the ground if your parachute doesn't open!

In reality, there's no real danger to seminar speaking. If you're feeling a little fear, just do it anyway! The rewards of seminar speaking far outweigh the risks.

"Musica Delenit Bestiam Feram."

There is research indicating that music is tied into the emotional circuitry of our brains. Music can definitely affect our moods. I would bet that you, like me, have songs that remind us of certain events or periods in our past.

What the heck does all this have to do with doing successful seminar speaking?

I'd like to suggest that at your events, you consider playing music before your seminar talk starts. You may want to consider playing music afterwards as well. Now, the style of music you play is up to you, of course, but I'd suggest you keep your target market in mind. If you'll be speaking to a group of mature seniors, then perhaps loud rock music might not be appropriate. Naturally, not every person in every group is going to like the same music. Since that's true, perhaps you might consider some "generic" classical or jazz music that serves more as background music until you start your talk.

I've found that some nice smooth music before and after an event sets a nice mood and tone. Try it and see for yourself!

Check the Pulse. Stat!

Do you check the pulse of your audience?

Of course, I don't mean that literally. I mean do you check in from time to time to see how "with you" your group is? There are several easy and effective ways to do this.

One is to sprinkle-in a little humor here and there and see if people are laughing. Another way is to ask them questions that elicit a response. Another is to give them a quick, small, specific task like having everyone write something down, or make a quick diagram that is part of you making a point. If you're doing a training or class of some type that involves the use of handouts or training materials, you can just look around and make sure that everyone is on the same page—literally!

If you don't occasionally take the pulse of your group, you run the risk of losing some or all of them. Don't get too far along in your talk before you start taking their pulse, then recheck along the way and you'll have everyone with you the whole way.

The Hero Process

Acting "natural" and seminar speaking. Isn't that a bit of an oxymoron? If you're being natural, then you're not acting, right? There are some who like to tell people that they should "act natural" when doing seminar speaking. They say that using what I call *The Hero Process* means you're not "being yourself".

That is just pure garbage! There's no way you can *not* be yourself. Everything you do, is you. If you pretend to be like someone else, it's YOU doing the pretending, right? Sorry, but you're pretty much stuck with you! You can't get away from the fact that you are you, period. Using my *Hero Process* only allows you to have more flexibility in your behaviors and increase your range of ability and skill as a seminar speaker. Notice I said *your* behavior and skill. Adding new behaviors and having more choices is always going to work in your favor, not work against you. Forget about that garbage advice to "act natural".

You already can act like yourself; that's no accomplishment. However, by learning from seminar speakers that are better than you, you can increase your skill. Seminar speaking is a skill just like golf or tennis is a skill; should you forget about taking golf lessons and just "act natural" on the golf course?

Get Curious to Get Unstuck

Sometimes we feel stuck. We feel like we're at an impasse about what to do or how to do it. Sometimes we feel like we have no good options—or no options at all. Here's how to get "unstuck" and get moving again.

The first step is to take a big step back. Taking a step back means removing yourself from the situation. If you're sitting, stand up and look back at the chair where you were sitting and step into a completely objective place.

Then, become curious: become curious about this situation, have the kind of curiosity that an investigator like Sherlock Holmes would have. Be intensely curious about this situation.

Then, get creative: start to generate alternatives and options on how to get unstuck and on the right track. Just generate a bunch of options without judging them, just generate as many as you can.

After that, evaluate the options you've generated and pick the one that feels best, and take action on it. Go for it. Just do it.

Use these steps like a recipe to get yourself unstuck anytime you need more options about any aspect of your seminar speaking.

Group Flow

When people get together and form into a group, there a number of different group dynamics that come into play. A major group dynamic to know about is the *stages of group flow*.

The first stage is when the group forms. That stage is characterized by initial confusion about what's happening.

The second stage is a result of the initial forming process and is a "stormy" stage where people begin to establish roles or rules. "You're sitting in my seat" is a small example of this stormy stage.

Once the storm has passed, the group settles into a rhythm in stage three. They begin to see themselves as part of the whole and are more cooperative.

There is a fourth stage very similar to stage three where the group is not only cooperating, but are now able to solve problems easily as they occur. They are operating at maximum efficiency and synergy in stage four.

Stage five is when the group breaks up and dissolves.

These stages can be subtle or overt, can cycle more than once, or even skip stages. But knowing about the five stages of group flow can be absolutely invaluable to your seminar success because you'll better understand the behavior and dynamics of your groups.

Sign, Sign, Everywhere a Sign!

Has this ever happened to you? You go to a seminar of some sort, drive to the venue, park, enter the building, then wander around for 20 minutes trying to figure out where the seminar room is?

If I had a dollar for every time that's happened to me, I'd have a room full of dollars! Sometimes even in a nice hotel it's hard to figure out where the heck the seminar room is. That's very frustrating—and it's even more frustrating when you walk into the seminar late after it's already started, when you were actually there early but finding the room turned into a new career!

Just recently, I arrived at a seminar location, found the address, but finding the room required psychic ability! How annoying!

Don't annoy and frustrate your seminar attendees. Put out plenty of signage to give clear direction as to where to go. Most venues like hotels will be able to assist you easily with that. You can even put a staff member out front to hold a sign with your seminar title so that arriving attendees will know that person is there to send them in the right direction.

Help your seminar attendees to easily get where their going. They'll appreciate it—and so will you when you don't have a room full of frustrated late arrivals!

A Feedback Sandwich

Here's a technique that can be very useful to you as a seminar speaker when you're conducting a workshop, class or training where you or others will be offering evaluations ("feedback") to the other participants. This technique is useful because it provides a structure and framework in which the person receiving the feedback is more likely to be receptive.

In other words, the *feedback sandwich technique* lowers the natural resistance people have to "criticism" even when that criticism is constructive. Here's how you do it:

First, tell them something specific that they did right.

Second, tell them something specific they need to do to improve.

Third, finally, give them a brief overall positive statement.

The "criticism" is sandwiched between two positive statements, making it more palatable to the recipient, in turn making it more likely they'll act on your suggestions for improvement.

Mr. and Mrs. Opposite

Occasionally, you may run into a situation where you have a seminar attendee who wants to disagree with everything you say. You say up, they say down. You say hot, they say cold. This person seems to start every sentence with "Yes, but..." and then want to contradict what you just said.

There are a number of ways to deal with this type of person. Here are a couple of my favorites that I've used with good success.

One way is to make them my own personal expert. I say something, and I turn to them and say "In 10 seconds or less, where would you disagree with what I just said?" Usually after calling on them a couple of times, they don't want to be called on anymore—and the audience is on my side.

Another way is to start with "Some of you may not agree with this..." and gesture in their direction while you look in a different direction.

Those two techniques work very well, and if you need more ideas on handling "Mr. or Mrs. Opposite" feel free to contact me via my website email.

The Abstraction Continuum of Language...WHAT?!?!

There are two very useful ways to think about how you use words and language. In the most simple terms, language and words exist along a range—or a continuum—of relative abstraction and specificity. In other words, you can be *vague* or you can be *specific* with the words you choose to use.

For example, saying "tree" is a lot less specific than "pine tree". If I'm speaking and I say "I was walking among the trees" then the listener doesn't know if I'm talking about maple trees, palm trees, or oak trees.

The more vague you are, the more you force the listener to create and make up mental representations in their head to understand what you're saying. The more specific you are, the less "creating" they have to do. Being vague tends to create a more "trance-like" state in your audience due to all the mental representations they have to make up; whereas being more specific tends to pull them more into the here and now and be more present mentally.

Knowing about the abstraction continuum of language can help you to decide how you want to use language to affect the mental state of your audience when you're doing seminar speaking.

How to Say "You Suck" Politely

Here's a technique that's just a bit more advanced than the "Feedback Sandwich" technique. In cases where you're conducting classes or trainings, you or others may be giving "criticism" or feedback to the other participants. Like the feedback sandwich, this more advanced technique makes criticism and feedback more palatable and more likely to be acted upon by the recipient. There are 4 parts to this feedback:

First, tell them something specific they did right or well.

Second, tell them what needs to be improved.

Third, ask them how they think they can improve.

Fourth, ask them how they'll do it different next time.

This kind of feedback is especially useful when your attendees are engaging in some kind of activity that you are offering feedback on. The fourth part of this feedback requires the participant to go out into the future and create in their mind how they'll do better the next time, which puts their mind on the right track for improving in the future.

Using the feedback sandwich and this more advanced technique "softens" the criticism making it much more likely that they will take your advice and act on your feedback.

Mark Your Spot

Here's an extremely sophisticated and highly effective technique for predictably controlling your audience's mood and reactions. This is an advanced staging technique very few people even know about, much less utilize. This technique involves "marking out" several spots on the floor or stage that represent specific emotional states you want your audience to be in. For example, let's say that you mark out three spots: one is front and center, one is 5 feet to the left of front and center, and one is 5 feet to the right. Let's say you assign front and center as your "sweet spot" where you'll deliver most of your talk. Left of that is your "funny" spot, where you'll stand every time you tell a funny story or joke. The right-of-center spot will be your "telling secrets" spot where you'll reveal inside information.

Those are just examples; you can designate various spots to represent whatever states you want your group to be in when you stand there.

Be sure to cleanly sort these spots before you give your talk; you can draw a diagram of the stage area and mark out what spots will represent which specific states. Once you start, don't mix them up!

The Cliffhanger

How would you like to be able to rivet audience attention and keep them hanging on your every word?

There are a number of ways I teach you to do this, and here's one of my favorites. I call it *The Cliffhanger*.

Have you ever watched a TV show where the season ends with a dramatic ending, but one where you have to tune in next season to find out what happens next? It's called a cliffhanger, and you can use those in your seminar speaking to your advantage.

A terrific way to use cliffhangers is to tell some story near the beginning of your seminar talk, but at the most dramatic part of the story, break away from the story and say something like "I'll finish that story later, but now let's talk about..." and shift to a different subject or the topic you came to speak about. Then, at the end of your talk, you pick up your story right where you left off at the dramatic break and finish the story. Cliffhangers keep people wondering the whole time how the story will resolve, so it rivets their attention to your talk.

Cliffhangers also keep people there for your whole talk because they don't want to leave and never get to find out how your dramatic story concludes.

Moving Vs. Standing

Should you speak from a podium, or should you move about the stage or the audience as you speak?

Ideally you want to be skilled at both, because each has definite advantages and disadvantages. You need to be good at both because if you're a "mover" you may be uncomfortable if you're ever forced to speak from a stationary microphone at a podium. And of course the opposite is true, too—if you're used to gripping or hiding behind a podium and there isn't one you may feel ill at ease. Especially when it's not your seminar and equipment and you're speaking at a convention or association meeting, you'll have no control over the stage set up or sound equipment. They may have cordless mics that allow you to move, or they may have only a stationary mic at the podium. Being facile and comfortable with both situations is best.

Podiums can be an advantage when the podium is perceived as "the place the experts talk from", but moving around the stage allows you to use my special staging techniques, as well as better interaction with the crowd.

There are definitely advantages to both situations, so you need to become comfortable with any room set up you encounter.

Making Your Point

Making your point clear is crucial to speaking success. I'm reminded of the saying *There is more than one road to the top of the mountain.* But no matter how you get there, the idea is to get to the top of the mountain. So, while certainly it's up to you how you choose to make your points clear, you must make your points clear.

A terrific way to do that is by using common, familiar expressions that make your point. Colloquialisms can achieve this end very nicely. There may also be certain specific expressions that your niche target market uniquely understands and uses, and that you can borrow to make your point. Sure, you can make your point by saying it directly, but if you can sum up your point in a familiar expression, it's more memorable to your audience.

An example of this is *This won't cost you much* versus *This won't cost you an arm and a leg.* Which is more memorable? Clearly the second expression stands out more in your mind because you've heard it on innumerable occasions and you know exactly what it means.

Be on the lookout for common expressions or colloquialisms that are evocative and memorable, and use them in your seminar speaking to help make your point clear and memorable.

The Cylinders Technique

Here's a simple technique to eliminate that nervous, awkward pacing many rookie speakers do. This technique is called the *Cylinders Technique.*

Think of your body parts each consisting of a single cylinder. Your arms, legs, torso, neck and head are each a single cylinder. Now, stand and line up your cylinders so no cylinder is out of balance—no cylinder is leaning forward or backward or sideways. Line up your leg cylinders underneath your torso cylinder, under your neck and head cylinders. Make everything line up. Line up all your cylinders, and feel the solid base you have. Feel how when all the cylinders are lined up, you can let your energy settle down through your feet and you feel solid and confident.

Now practice some of your seminar talk in this solid, confident position.

By becoming solidly grounded like that, you will gain confidence and lose the awkward, nervous pacing.

Projection

Are you ready for another time-tested and proven technique to quickly and easily develop your vocal ability?

It's been my experience after teaching literally thousands of people how to improve their presentation skills, that a huge concern many people have is about their voice. Specifically, their ability to project their voice. Here's a terrific method to improve your vocal projection.

You're going to make a series of sounds, not words. First, put your lips together and make an "MMMM" sound. Then, without stopping, part your lips and make an "AHHH" sound. Continue with an "OHHH" sound, then an "OOOO" sound, and finally an "EEEE" sound. Then take a nice deep breath and repeat it.

As you repeat, start to feel it getting stronger, but be sure not to tense your throat and neck muscles, let those muscles remain loose and relaxed. As you continue to repeat, notice that you can increase the resonation of each sound and that you can make it louder with that resonation. Allow the sound to emanate more from the front of your face instead of your throat. Finally, imagine that you can project your voice across the room to the outside of the opposite wall.

Stay relaxed and loose the whole time you do this. Soon you'll feel a measurable improvement in your vocal ability.

You Think They Can!
You Think They Can!

A peculiar dynamic of seminar speaking— group events of almost *any* type, really—is the way people subconsciously absorb the beliefs of the speaker. This is especially true in a class or training environment where the student has elected to participate through a desire to learn about the subject.

In such cases, the student electing to participate in the training, generally speaking, would not be there if they thought the class or training was bogus or ineffective. This faith that the student puts in the instructor/teacher/trainer means that the student is absorbing the inherent beliefs that the instructor holds. Why is this important?

Because if you're training a group, and you're holding a belief that this group is not able to grasp or absorb what you're imparting, you will essentially "make this come true". It's just like the proverbial self-fulfilling prophecy.

Whether it's true or not, it's much more practical and effective to hold the belief steady in your mind that your group is able to learn and absorb what you're teaching them.

Today Only: FREE Money!

Should you give away cash at your seminar?

This is definitely not appropriate to all seminar speaking engagements. However, this is a tactic that really gets people's attention. This technique is used in a lot of "get rich quick" seminars to rivet the attention of the audience. Here's how it works: Near the beginning of the talk the seminar speaker will ask a question, and the first person to raise their hand is given cash, usually $10 or $20. The seminar speaker makes it clear that the reason this person is receiving cash is because they were the first to raise their hand. Now everyone is ready to raise their hand quickly in hopes of being the next person to get cash. Sure enough, several minutes later the speaker asks another question, and the person with the first hand up is given cash. The speaker elaborates saying that s/he likes to reward those who take action quickly and are paying attention.

Of course, this technique is a blatant manipulation tactic because at the end of the seminar, when the sales pitch comes, the speaker repeats that only people who act quickly will reap benefits (like making more money).

This tactic may sound trite and shallow, but cash really gets people's attention. In my opinion, giving away cash is not recommended for most seminar situations, but ultimately you'll have to decide for yourself.

T'an T'ien

The *T'an T'ien* is a Chinese term referring to a spot on your abdomen located about two or three finger widths below your belly button. The *t'an t'ien* is thought of as the place where universal energy is concentrated.

Now, this technique does not require that you believe in universal energy. It works no matter what your beliefs are. Here's how it works: imagine that universal energy can flow into the top of your head and fill up your body like water pouring into a glass. It helps to imagine this energy having a color like gold, silver, pure white light, or your favorite color. It can even be rainbow-like if you prefer. Now, imagine that this energy fills up your body so full that is overflows out through your *t'an t'ien* and fills up the room, touching everyone in the room.

If nothing else, this technique allows you to feel connected to your audience which can eliminate stage fright and anxiety because these people are not a bunch of strangers separate from you—they are all "connected" to you!

Short & Simple, Stupid!

Be brief.

In this case I'm specifically referring to bullet points in your handouts and especially projected onto a screen. Rookie presenters will put *way too many* bullet points on a single slide. I've seen that many times in seminars I've gone to. It's too much information for one slide, it overwhelms people, and they shut down and stop paying attention.

Now, if your aim is to get people to stop paying attention, then you're on the right track. However, I bet you want people actually awake and aware of your seminar talk.

Keep your bullet points short and brief. Make them concise and memorable. After all, that's the whole point of bullet points. Limit yourself to *ten* bullet points per screen *at the most*, but only display one at a time so you can focus the group's attention on the point you're making, and so they don't read ahead and not listen to you.

Remember, short sentences and phrases are more easily absorbed. And, they're more easily remembered.

What About...The Other Guy?

Occasionally in the workshops and seminars I teach such as my ***Seminar Speaking Success Mastery*** boot camps, someone will ask what they should do about competition. They usually want to know how to set themselves apart from anyone else who's doing seminars that might be competing with their seminars.

First, most of your competitors are not going to be doing seminars, and even if they are, it's likely their seminars are not very good. Most speakers are untrained and don't know how to properly format and deliver their talk. Just by using the information I teach you, you'll be way ahead of your competition.

Perhaps more importantly is your mindset about competition: Are you creating some kind of barrier in your mind that there is this "competition" out there that stops you from moving forward? Sometimes it's as if we view the world through a pane of glass, and something gets "stuck" on the glass and we see the whole world filtered through that one thing. Do you have "there's so much competition" stuck on your view of the world?

If you're worried about competition, the best thing you can do is just move forward, focus on the targets you want to hit, and stop focusing on what the competition is doing.

It Ain't Over Until…

This is where some speakers, especially beginners, really fall apart. They don't know how to end their talk. They don't know how to close the seminar and get off the stage (or leave the front of the room). The end of their talk will trail off in some weak drivel and no one is sure what's happening—they're not sure if they should clap, leave, or what.

Don't make that mistake.

The end of your seminar should be two parts:

One, tell them what action you want them to take, and two, say "thank you" and leave the stage.

The first part is so critical. Tell people what you want them to do! Are you offering a free appointment in your office? Tell them to go to the back table and make an appointment. Do you want them to fill out and turn in an order form for your product? Tell them to turn in their order forms at the back table. Do you want them to meet you in a different room for a private break-out session? Tell them where to go and what time to be there. Tell them exactly what action they're supposed to take next, say "thank you", and you're officially done.

Don't blow a great presentation or seminar talk by not knowing how to stop talking!

Applause, Please!

Would you like people to give you a nice round of applause at the end of your seminar talk? Here's a technique that works very well. You're actually going to give the audience a cue that it's time for them to start clapping at the end of your talk.

Right before you're about to stop talking and end with "thank you", you hold your hands out away from your body toward the audience, hands slightly wider than your shoulders and about chest level. Both hands are palm up facing the ceiling. As you're saying "thank you", you bring your hands together close to your body, about level with your solar plexus area and clasp your hands. This give everyone a non-verbal cue that it's time to clap.

People will want to give you a nice round of applause at the end of your talk, and you're doing them a service by giving them a subtle cue that this is their chance to do it.

Don't deprive your audience of the opportunity and pleasure of giving you a hearty round of applause. They want to do it—and you deserve it!

Oh, End It Already!

In reality, there is no one right way to close your seminar talk. I do highly recommend, however, that you make your close a *call to action* where you tell your group what you want them to do.

However, that may not be appropriate for your specific class, workshop, training, seminar, or conference. Another terrific way to close a group event is to tell a story that wraps up and encapsulates your topic and your message, especially if that story carries a lot of emotional weight, or is particularly inspirational.

Like it or not, people tend to remember the last thing they heard. So another factor to consider is what do you want them have at the top of their mind as they're leaving? The emotional story close is great if you want them to leave feeling moved and/or inspired. If you're selling something, you probably want them leaving with your product or, at the very least, your order form—and good reasons to buy!

Once you've designed whatever your close will be, switch places and imagine you have attended your own seminar and ask yourself if the end of your talk is producing the results you want to get.

Be My Guest

Are you using guest speakers at your seminar?

There are many advantages to having a guest speaker at your seminar, not the least of which is having them share in the costs, which reduces your out of pocket expenses. Another major advantage is the added value to your seminar when you've got an expert speaking on something of value to your group, but is outside your area of expertise. Having a guest speaker also breaks up the monotony of just one speaker, just one face, just one voice the whole time.

If you do have a guest speaker, be sure that you agree in advance on some key areas. For example, how long do they get to speak? What signal will you give them when they're near the end of their time limit? If they're to help with expenses, how much will that be exactly? Will they be allowed to overtly sell their product or service to your group? If so, will there be a split of the profit? Also, you should review an outline of their talk ahead of time to make sure that there's nothing in there you wouldn't want brought up at your seminar.

Having guest speakers can provide value to your seminar. But, be 100% clear with yourself and them in advance about what the "rules" are. That will make sure you don't end up with any unpleasant surprises later.

"Don't Shoot Until You See The Whites of Their Eyes!"

That was said by Major William Prescott. Perhaps we should modify the saying to "Don't *speak* until you see the whites of their eyes."

Making eye contact with your group is definitely a good thing. If you're speaking in a giant auditorium with a spotlight on you, you won't be able to make out much more than the first or second row of people. Even then, it's a good idea to look into your crowd as if you can see them.

However, in most cases it's likely you'll be able to see the faces of pretty much everyone there. A time-tested and proven eye-contact technique is to shift your gaze from person to person every couple of sentences. If you have already practiced speaking with your eyes defocused (highly recommended) then you can shift your gaze to various sections at a time, and that will give the illusion of eye contact. Avoid looking over people's heads. But don't avoid making any eye contact at all because that creates a disconnect between you and your audience.

Finally, don't stare at any one person for too long because that can make them feel uncomfortable.

Who Cares?

Does your seminar talk pass the *Who Cares?* test?

The *Who Cares? test* is a nice little acid-test for your overall seminar talk. As you can likely guess, the *Who Cares?* test is geared to get you out of your head, out of your opinions about your seminar talk, and put yourself into other people's shoes. YOU may care greatly about your topic, but don't assume that just because you do that others will, too. You may be surprised to find out that you have to make people care about your topic. You may think that real estate, insurance, retirement planning, health issues (or whatever your topic is) is something that everyone cares about.

You have to be brutally honest with yourself and your seminar talk and ask yourself would the average person actually care about your topic based solely on what you have to say in your seminar talk?

Look at the title of your talk and ask yourself, "Who cares?" Look over your main points and ask yourself, "Who cares?"

Does your seminar title and talk pass the *Who Cares? test*?

This Tip is NOT About Gardening

Does your seminar talk focus on the *lawnmower* or the *lawn*? This tip is not about gardening and landscaping, just in case you were wondering. The real questions here is, does your talk talk focus more on the features of your product and/or service or does it focus more on the benefits your audience will get.

If your talk is more about "the lawnmower" than the "lawn," you may want to change that. Your "lawnmower" may be the newest, best, most high-tech creation ever. It may have a jet engine, do 150 miles per hour, and have an onboard computer. Yawn.

Those are just features of the lawnmower. Instead of focusing on features, focus on *benefits to the user*. What will that great lawnmower do for ME? Will it mow the lawn perfectly by itself while I lie in a hammock enjoying a glass of lemonade? Will all my neighbors be jealous of how beautiful my lawn is? Will it save me time? Will it save me money?

You may be selling the best lawnmower in the world, but people are much more interested their lawn than your lawnmower!

In the Blink of an Eye

You have much less time than you think you have. This is not a philosophical discussion about how much time we have in our lives. Rather, this is a very practical fact about your seminar talk.

You don't have as much time for your seminar talk as you think you do. All beginners worry that they have too much time and not enough material to fill the time. The opposite is always true. You have less time than you think you do. Many beginners then find when they deliver their first few seminars that they have too much material for the time allotted for them to speak. This is a mistake that even many seasoned pros make because our natural tendency is to feel that we don't have enough information to fill up the time.

Naturally, it's better to have too much information rather than too little, but my experience has been that people rarely mind if you finish a few minutes early.

Don't worry that you have too much time and not enough material, the opposite is true more often than not!

Three Essential Skills

Conducting any kind of group event like seminars, public speaking, workshops, and so forth require skills in three main areas:

1. Conquering stage fright/fear of public speaking.
This is vital, because this is what stops most people from doing any seminar speaking in the first place, and reaping the many rewards. Those people might as well rip up $100 bills every day.

2. Seminar logistics.
Seminars and workshops and group events of all types require attention to 1,001 details. If you don't know how to handle those myriad details, your seminar will be a painful, chaotic ordeal.

3. Presentation and stage skills.
You absolutely must know how to structure your talk properly—or else you're completely wasting your time. And, you must be able to deliver your talk with masterful presentation skills—or your whole seminar will simply fall flat.

My company, *The American Seminar Academy* will train and teach you on all three of these important levels. Be sure to go to *www.SeminarAcademy.com* and sign up for the next workshop.

Take Out the Trash

Are you using "junk" and 'garbage" words and phrases? You already know to weed out all the *umms* and *uhhs* from your seminar speaking. But what about overused words and phrases? Those need to go, too. Words like "actually" are often quite overused. So is "basically". Actually, those words basically are not adding anything to your seminar talk.

Other overused phrases include "to tell you the truth", "you know", and "to be honest with you".

Those words and phrases are what I call "junk" and "garbage" words and phrases. They don't add anything to your seminar talk, and in fact they detract from it.

Actually, to tell you the truth, you basically need to weed those "junk" and "garbage" words and phrases from your vocabulary—just to be honest with you—you know?

Use the Force…

Have you ever seen those martial arts movies where they blindfold the student and then the master starts throwing punches and kicks at the blindfolded student, who then blocks them with ease? Believe it or not, this does have its real-life counterpart in some martial arts training—and it does have something to do with seminar speaking.

Here's what I mean: When you're giving a talk, keep your eyes open but let them defocus when you speak. This allows you an *expanded awareness* of everything going on in your seminar. In fact, the famous Kalahari Bushmen hunters use this technique when hunting and they can easily detect even the slightest movement in the brush.

In your seminar speaking, you won't be blindfolded or hunting, but it's useful to be able to expand your awareness to your entire group. You'll pick up on subtle changes that you'd otherwise miss. Try it, and you'll see what I mean!

Is It Live Or Is It ...

You should strongly consider recording one of your seminar talks and there are a number of terrific reasons why.

One really great use for your audio is to make it your "hold music" on your office line. When someone calls your office, instead of hearing boring and bland hold music, they're listening to you!

Another truly terrific thing to do is to take the audio and burn CDs (or whatever the current medium is since technology changes so fast) and give those away just like business cards. In fact, give people a business card and your audio CD. Now that's impressive! People will listen to it, copy it for friends, and of course it promotes you and your business.

You can upload the audio to your website for visitors to listen to as well.

Finally, you can make your audio available as a product to purchase either via website download or as a physical product you sell at future seminar talks.

Making an audio recording of your talk is a terrific idea that can pay dividends over and over.

Free Publicity

I highly recommend using the media and getting publicity to promote your seminars. Free seminars have a more likely chance to be published in your local paper than paid seminars because reporters may feel that you should be advertising instead of getting publicity. To get your publicity campaign going, you don't need to hire expensive PR firms. All you have to do is write a press release and send it to your local media, such as newspapers and radio stations. You can find tons of free info on the internet on how to write and send press releases, and in my audio CD *Power Publicity* I go into a lot of detail about exactly how to get free publicity to promote your business and your seminars, and you can find out more about that at *www.SeminarAcademy.com*.

It's not rocket science and you definitely don't need to hire PR firms. You can do it all yourself quickly, easily, and inexpensively.

Getting publicity for your seminar talks also helps to elevate you as the expert on your topic. After all, you wouldn't be in the media if you weren't the expert, right?

Chutes & Ladders

Does the business of seminar speaking have a "corporate ladder" that you have to climb starting at the bottom? The one word answer is no. Seminar speaking is a business and industry that does not have a "ladder" you have to climb to get somewhere.

At the same time, it's good advice to walk before you run. That means you may want to get your feet wet with some smaller seminars before you go after bigger ones. Doing smaller seminars at first allows you to work out the kinks in your presentation, make sure you're bullet proof with any technology you're using, and work out any lingering nervousness or anxiety about public speaking.

That being said, you can jump into the industry anywhere you're ready and prepared to do so. If you want to go for the top speaking gigs in the country by contacting big event promoters, go right ahead. Again, having a track record will be in your favor, but there's no hard and fast prerequisites you'll have to have even if you're going after the big time right out the gate.

No, there is no corporate ladder to climb when it comes to seminar speaking—and that's to your advantage!

We Want ... Information

How should you keep track of all the information about the people who attend your seminars?

Some people I know just keep all the data on all their seminars and who attended in a paper notebook. I find it easier to use a database or spreadsheet program for that. One of the reasons to use a database or spreadsheet program is ease of looking up, sorting, and printing information. It's up to you how much data and detail you want to track, but clearly each person's contact information, which seminar they attended, when they attended and where is some of the basic info you want to keep.

Another reason to keep a database is for the all-important purposes of follow up. You can follow up with special offers, sales pitches, or just even a thank you card.

Keeping a database does not have to turn into a new career. Just pick the method that works best for you and remember that you can always modify your database later.

My Old School

Your topic may be perfect for booking speaking engagements at schools. Consider your local community college, university, or even elementary school as potential places to spread your message. If you're scratching your head as to how you could "fit" into any kind of agenda at a school, just contact the school and ask if they have a need for someone to come in and speak on your topic, business, or industry. They'll typically know right away if they can make use of your topic. They may have a "career day" or similar program where you'd fit right in. Or they may want you to speak to their job placement department. Maybe your topic or talk is motivational and inspirational, which could be a big hit and you have the additional gratifying feeling knowing that you may just impact some young people's lives in a positive way.

Keep in mind, that not only students are going to hear your talk and become aware of you, your business, and your message. There will likely be teachers, administrators, and perhaps even parents who'll be there, too.

Your Promo Package

Do you need a promotional package including video, bio, and professionally photographed headshots?

If you're using seminar speaking to promote your business, your message, or to position yourself as the expert in your community, then you won't need to have a promo package.

If, on the other hand, you plan on being represented by an agency or bureau, they'll want you to have video, headshots, and a slick promo package so they can shop you around. There's no shortage of agencies, bureaus, and businesses that will be glad to charge you many hundreds or probably even thousands of dollars to put together a slick promo package for you. If you're just starting out, you're more likely to think you have to have all that stuff to appear credible. However, if you are just starting out, I'd recommend you not spend money on a promo package. Get your feet wet doing some real speaking and get a track record established before you even consider spending money on a promo package.

I also recommend that you get some training if you're just starting out so you save yourself a lot of wasted time and energy re-inventing the wheel. I suggest you look at my workshops at *www.SeminarAcademy.com* where I offer a number of comprehensive workshops, products, trainings, and coaching.

Let's Hit the Clubs!

Here's another terrific way to promote your business and spread your message quickly and easily with seminar speaking:

Try contacting some of the "specialty clubs" in your area. What is a specialty club? Glad you asked. Here are some examples—

auto enthusiast clubs, scuba diving clubs, investment clubs, singles clubs, garden clubs, art clubs, photography clubs

Get the idea?

This is different than the Rotary, Elk's and clubs of that nature. Specialty clubs are clubs where the members all share a common interest. It's very likely that the organizers of these clubs are looking for something different to add some spice to their meetings. Even if you don't scuba dive or have a garden, the club may be thrilled to have you there and speak. If they think your topic is not of interest, or interferes with any of the members existing businesses, they'll let you know.

Check with your local chamber of commerce for a list of the clubs in your area, then start making some phone calls. The worst that can happen is they say "no", but chances are you'll book some gigs.

The Library

Did you know that you can speak at your local library, and that you get to use the room for free? Did you also know that they'll help promote your seminar? They'll put out fly-ers promoting your seminar. And yes, you will get to use the room for free. To be fair, some libraries in some cities do charge for use of their room, but a great many do not charge at all.

What's the catch? Simply this: You may not charge a fee for attending your seminar and your topic must be of inter-est and benefit to your community. And you won't be able to sell anything at your seminar. If you have trouble figuring out how to adjust your topic and talk to fit community inter-est and benefit, just contact me and I'll help you with that, it's really quite easy to do.

Even though you can't charge a fee or sell anything at your seminar, you can pass out handouts, business cards, brochures, flyers, and other promotional material.

Free seminars always have their advantages and disad-vantages, but booking a seminar talk at the local library is a terrific way to spread your message, help the community, and gain valuable experience in seminar speaking.

Hard or Soft?

Is your topic a *hard topic* or a *soft topic*? Do you know the difference?

Generally speaking, hard topics are about tangibles such as financial planning, how to prepare your will, or how to purchase real estate. Soft topics are about intangibles such as motivation, inspiration, or overcoming adversity. Which category does your topic and talk fall into?

Are soft topics "better" than hard topics? Or is it vice versa? Some would say that hard topics are better, because it's usually easier to sell something tangible such as real estate or investments. But in actuality, that's a judgment call that only you can make. Why? Because a soft topic can have huge appeal to people. Your story of overcoming all the odds and coming out on top could find a wide audience and be very successful.

Being clear about whether you have a soft topic or a hard topic can help you to better select your audiences and your seminar speaking opportunities and engagements.

Seminar Super Success Formula

There's no one set way, one perfect way to structure the sequence of your seminar talk. The sequence and structure ultimately depends on what you're trying to accomplish. What works in a teaching and training context may fall flat in a marketing, promotional, or selling context.

One very good sequence is based on my *Seminar Super Success Formula*. Here's a condensed summary of that sequence: introduction, thank you and welcome, logistics, set ground rules, establish purpose and reason for being there, outline the problems you can help them solve, outline how you solve those problems, link the solutions to you, give testimonials, make a call to action, then close.

You can see that if your seminar is purely instructional and educational in nature, this might not work best in that context. If you're purely educating then you'd want to use one of the other presentation structuring techniques I teach you like "open loops", "linked modules", and "pre-teaching".

Ultimately you should use a structure you like and that you are comfortable with, because your comfort and confidence key.

Getting to Know You

People buy from and do business with people they like, believe, and trust. That's an established fact. Seminar speaking is the perfect way for people to get to know you and form an opinion about you. The *introductory evening seminar* is the perfect way for you to let people get to know you.

Create a title for your introductory seminar, one that's irresistible to your target market or at least that gets their attention and makes them want to know more. Hold a free 1½—2 hour seminar on that topic. You can hold it in your office if you have space, although people might feel more comfortable going to a "neutral" location like the library or hotel meeting room. During your seminar, give out a lot of information on your topic. Loosen up and don't be so stiff, have some fun, just be who you are and enjoy it. If you're having fun, so will your seminar attendees.

At the end, pass out some free information and, of course, your brochures and other information about you and your business. You can also offer free consultations if appropriate.

An introductory evening is the perfect venue for people to get to know you, like you, and believe you—all of which translates to them doing business with you!

God Is in the Details

If you're new to doing seminar speaking and organizing your own seminars, you'll quickly find that there are a million-and-one details to attend to. It can be truly overwhelming. In my *Quick Start Seminar Success System*, I lay out step-by-step exactly what to do and when to do it so you can handle all those details with ease and the peace of mind that you're not forgetting anything important—especially when just one missed detail can mean total chaos and disaster.

When planning your seminars, think of it in three phases. First phase is pre-planning, which includes all your prep work such as venue, handouts, seminar title, date and time, and structuring your presentation and marketing plan. Phase two is everything that will happen at your seminar, who will do what and when and how things will flow. Phase three is seminar follow up, how exactly will you follow up with your seminar attendees? Will you be providing coaching? Mailing sales letters? Sending thank you cards?

Seminars are the fastest, easiest, and most fun way to promote and grow your business, but they can quickly spin out of control unless you make sure you're on top of a myriad of crucial details.

Plan your seminar details carefully!

Will That Be All?

Make it easy for people to register for your seminar. If you will have a registration form on your website, make it simple and easy to find and use. In most cases, you'll also be taking phone registrations, which means you have to think about some details such as...

What phone number will you give out for people to call? Will someone be able to answer that number 24 hours a day? Many times people will call after business hours and you stand to lose registrations unless you can register them when they do call. If you're not going to have a service of live operators, then your voicemail had better be 100% clear to the caller that they can register via voicemail. If people call during business hours, is your staff clear on how to handle that?

If you don't capture their phone number and other important contact information at that time, you can't get a hold of them in case of cancellation or rescheduling of your seminar. Will you be taking payment over the phone?

I suggest you put together a seminar phone registration form for you and your staff to use when someone calls to register. Have blank spaces to fill in name, contact info, and so forth. Also have a mini checklist right there on the form so your staff doesn't forget to inform the registrants about parking or other important info they'll need.

Let Them Handle It

If you'd like to do a lot of seminar speaking but want to leave the details to someone else, then you might want to use a speakers bureau. If you just want to show up and speak (and cash a check) this could be a good way for you to go. You can uncover a ton of them with a quick Internet search.

Most speakers bureaus will want to see a promotional package of some sort. Requirements will vary from bureau to bureau, but they'll typically want a bio with your background and experience on your topic, a good head shot of you, and usually a demo video of some sort. Many bureaus will help you to put all that together, for a fee. You can do much of this on your own, however, and probably save some money too. The advantage of using a bureau is that they'll probably be fairly well-connected, and have a number of people coming to them looking for speakers. Of course, the bureau will collect the speaking fee, and then pay you your cut.

Using a speakers bureau can be advantageous since they'll do the marketing part, and you'll do the speaking part. Check it out and decide if a speaker's bureau is right for you.

National Organizations

There are a number of national organizations that cater to speakers. Each of them will have a local chapter you can contact. These organizations are essentially clubs and associations that are comprised of speakers with varying levels of experience. Some clubs cater mostly to beginners.

Others only allow experienced seminar speakers to join. My experience is that these organizations mostly provide a group of like-minded individuals that you can connect with.

You'll have to decide for yourself if these organizations are of benefit to you or not. That depends on what you're trying to accomplish. For sure these organizations will provide camaraderie which can help bolster your resolve and keep you moving on the path.

You will have to pay dues to belong to any of these organizations, so you'll want to attend a meeting or two for free first to see if you really want to join their club or not.

Goin' Corporate

One path to consider as a seminar speaker is speaking in the corporate market. You may want to contact companies that are likely candidates to use your product or service. An educational seminar or training may be something they need or want. Also, large companies will hold annual parties and want to hire speakers. These events are perfect for motivational and inspirational speakers, as well as speakers that are humorous or entertaining.

Larger companies will employ the services of a speakers bureau, so if you're planning to crack the corporate market you may want to affiliate with one of the larger bureaus that cater to that market. Of course, you can market yourself directly to that market as well, but it's easier when you have a bureau selling you. But if you're looking to train and teach employees a certain skill, or to be more productive, you can certainly contact companies directly and pitch them on your classes and trainings.

Corporations often have a budget that includes money to bring in outside speakers and trainers, so be sure to consider the corporate market as a potential hot target market.

Born to Speak

It's been said that seminar speakers are born, not made. That's pure baloney, it's not true at all. Sure, some people are more of a "ham" than others and seem to desire the spotlight even from an early age. Becoming a polished professional seminar speaker is nothing less than a learned skill.

I can take a total beginner, someone riddled with stage fright and fear of public speaking, and turn them into a polished pro practically overnight. You weren't born knowing how to tie your shoes, sign your name, or drive a car, but you learned how. So if you have no idea how to conquer stage fright and fear of public speaking, you can rest assured it's much easier to do than you think.

Maybe you don't have any fear of public speaking or stage fright, but you don't have the foggiest idea of how to do seminars or structure a talk. Again, it's all skills you can learn, just like you learned to drive a car or ride a bike.

Never let anyone try to convince you that you can't do seminar speaking—you can become a polished pro quickly and easily—much faster than you can imagine!

Other Peoples' Contacts

When you speak at other people's events, how can you get the contact information of the attendees?

It's important to understand that when you go out and speak at other people's events, you want to leverage that opportunity and be able to follow up with the attendees. However, in many cases, you're simply not going to be given a list of each of the attendees and their contact info. And, you won't be able to just ask them all to give you their contact info. What to do?

Easy...hold a drawing!

Take a couple of your books, videos audio products or other items that have high perceived value. Tell everyone you're going to hold a drawing for valuable prizes at the end of your talk. The attendees enter by putting on of their business cards into a bag or hat or whatever, and you draw the winners by pulling out a business card. When you put your hand into the hat, mix up the cards and don't pull out anything that feels like a scrap of paper, only pull out what feels like a business card.

After the drawing, you keep all the business cards, and *voila*! You have everyone's contact info so you can follow up with them!

Extra! Extra! Read All About It!

Do you know how to get publicity for your seminars by sending out a press release?

You can find tons of press release templates online you can use as a model to follow. Realize that the most important aspect of your release is the headline—it simply must grab the readers attention. Spend 80% of your time on the headline. Make your press release one page only, double space typed, and at the bottom put # # # to indicate the end of the release.

Once your press release is ready to go, just fax it off to the local media. You can email it too, but experts disagree on this. The most important elements are that it does not look like an advertising piece, and your headline must grab the attention of the reader.

You can send out a simple announcement of your seminar, short and sweet. You may want to send out different releases over time since you might not get published on your very first press release.

Class...Class...Shut Up!

What should you do if some people just won't stop talking to each other during your seminar talk?

In other tips, I've advised you as to how to set ground rules at the start of your seminar to prevent this problem so you can nip it in the bud easily and with tact so that you don't alienate your group. But, what if you're speaking at someone else's event and there are a couple of people who just won't shut up?

The rookie speaker feels they have to "win them over". The rookie speaker will talk and look in their direction more than the rest of the group. The rookie speaker feels that they're failing unless they can get those two to shut up and listen. However, the seasoned pro knows that the two best choices are either make a funny and clever remark about it, or ignore it. The safest thing to do is just ignore them and talk to the people who *are* listening! My colleagues and students who've gone through this have all told me that they found out for themselves that it's a big mistake to try to play to and "win over" any people having a conversation while you're making your presentation.

Ignore them. Let someone else in the crowd tell them to shut up. Do not under any circumstances try to play to them, or give them more attention than the rest of the group, or try to "win them over". Just ignore them!

Half of This Game is 90% Mental

Yogi Berra said that and nothing can be more true. Especially when it comes to giving a seminar. Many people agonize over the idea of having to stand up in front of people and speak. But, once they start speaking, they quickly find they were blowing their fear way out of proportion. After you do some seminar speaking, you'll realize this is true.

However, until you get there, here's another tip to help you to conquer that pesky stage fright. Simply put, just visualize your audience as bathing in and surrounded by a white light. Imagine that light is the universal light of love and healing. It helps if you really put yourself into this and believe it's true. If you have strong religious faith, you can imagine that the white light is coming from God, Allah, or whatever name you call the Ultimate. Or you can use the generic "universal light" if you prefer.

The idea here is that you focus all your attention on the audience as being surrounded by love and light.

If this technique comes easy to you, great! If not, persist with it for a while and see what happens—sometimes the techniques that don't come easy at first end up being of the most help if you just keep trying!

Ummm...Ummm

One of the biggest fears, objections, and barriers people have to doing seminars and public speaking is the fear of getting stumped on a question from the audience.

When it comes to the reasons people have public speaking fear, this is a biggie. But with my help, you'll quickly realize that this is a non-existent "bogey man" and is not anything to fear. Here are some strategies on how to handle questions you don't know the answer to:

1. Tell them you'll answer that question personally later after the seminar.
2. Put your hand to your chin and say, "Hmm, that's a good question...let me get back to you later on that" and move on in your talk.
3. Tell them you want to be sure you fully and correctly answer their question and not give them a "snap" answer, so you'll get back to them later personally by phone or email.

Never appear flustered, just give them one of the above answers with a confident demeanor, move on, and you'll be fine.

Rookie speakers think they must know the answer to all possible questions or they'll look bad. Experienced pros, however, know that it just does not matter! Use the strategies I give you and you'll find out for yourself that this is true!

Woops!

What should you do if you trip, mumble, drop something, or make some other gaffe?

This is a major cause of stage fright and fear of public speaking in people. They're afraid they'll trip over something, spill the water, trip over their own words, or otherwise make a "mistake".

First of all, get over yourself and stop taking yourself so seriously. If you're trying to be perfect, stop it! Really! People will relate to you and like you better if you're human, just like them. If you try to be perfect and your attitude is stuffy, they won't like you much anyway.

Now, if you do make some kind of blunder, there are two simple, easy, effective choices: **ignore it** or **make a joke** about it.

If you spilled water on yourself, that's the perfect place to crack an off-the-cuff joke. Poking fun at yourself is "self-deprecating" humor and can be some of the funniest and useful humor there is. If you trip over something, it's another great opportunity to make a joke, or you can ignore it and just keep going.

Ignoring a mistake is the sign of a pro. If it's a mistake you can't ignore, then just laugh it off and keep going with your talk!

For Sale

Should you create a product or even a line of products to sell at your seminars?

Ostensibly, this will depend on your business, industry, and target market. Some industries, such as financial services and investments are very tightly regulated and you may need approval from the compliance department on anything you produce.

That being said, I'm hard pressed to think of a business or industry that would not benefit from having products. It's been my direct experience that people at seminars want to "take a part of you home with them" and pretty much expect products to be on sale. Remember, you don't have to sell your products, they can be given away in a drawing, or given out like business cards. Informational audio can be made and reproduced extremely inexpensively, and are quite impressive. You can make a collection of articles you've written into a 3-ring binder and give that away. You can film one of your seminars and create a video you give away or sell.

If you need more ideas or help, contact me via ***www. SeminarAcademy.com*** because I've got tons of resources you can use to make products quickly and inexpensively.

Have You Heard of the NSA?

No, not the National Security Administration. In this case, the NSA is the National Speaker's Association. Their membership may be limited to professional speakers, and you may be required to provide information about how many paid speaking engagements you've made over a certain time period. Membership in their organization will also mean you'll have to pay a membership fee. Some people really like belonging to organizations like the NSA because of the camaraderie and support they get, plus the educational presentations at the meetings. Other people find such organizations not of much use, but the final decision is, of course, up to you. It couldn't hurt to contact your local chapter and attend a free meeting one time and see how you like it. Just do an internet search and you'll turn their contact info up pretty quickly.

Personally, I recommend you train with the **American Seminar Academy** which you can contact at *www. SeminarAcademy.com*, but my opinion may be a little biased!

Need-to-Know Basis

If you're a veteran of seminar speaking, then you know that you can expect things to go wrong. You learn to expect it—equipment fails, your presentation notes mysteriously disappear, the room is much different than you expected, and so on.

If you're speaking at someone else's organization as opposed to putting on your own seminar, then you should send off a pre-talk questionnaire to your host to minimize unpleasant, unexpected surprises. Your questionnaire can be as little as one or two questions or it can be pages long. You can get a sample pre-talk questionnaire at *www. SeminarAcademy.com.* Customize yours to suit your needs. Some typical questions to get you in the right direction include:

- How many people will attend, what is their gender and profession?
- Is there any inside information or funny events that you should know about and refer to in your talk?
- Are there any subjects you should avoid?

Include any questions you have about the room, the equipment, who to contact when there, and so forth. As they say, "an ounce of prevention is worth a pound of cure" and your pre-talk questionnaire can save you pounds of pain later!

Easy "Entitlement"

Scan a newspaper or magazine, and look for headlines that catch your attention. The editor of that publication would not have let that headline and story run unless s/he thought it would be of interest to the readers. I suggest you clip and save a collection of headlines that are attention grabbing for future use.

As you look at headlines that capture your attention, pay close attention to the structure of the headline. Most headlines can be easily reworked to suit your topic. My local paper, for example, has a headline "7 Tips to Make Your Garden Greener".

All we need to do is replace some words with our topic. For example, a real estate agent could write "7 Tips to Avoid Overpaying for a Home". Financial planners could write "7 Tips to a Secure Retirement". Chiropractors could write "7 Tips to Solving Back Pain". See how easy that is?

Creating catchy titles for your seminar talk and your press releases is just that easy! Start looking through some newspapers starting right now!

Differences

What really is the difference between a seminar, workshop, boot camp, conference, summit, symposium, class, training, or meeting?

What they all share in common is that a group (or audience if you prefer) are gathered to hear a person or persons speak on some specific topic or topics. Setting aside dictionary definitions, the most important difference between those terms are how they affect the listener psychologically.

My research and surveys indicate that people respond quite favorably to the words *workshop, conference, seminar, training,* and even *"get together"*. In general the word *seminar* seems to convey that a speaker will be mostly presenting, whereas a *workshop* seems to indicate that the group will be involved in some activity, and not just passively listening to a speaker. *Conferences, summits, symposiums,* and *meetings* seem to convey that there will be discussion and an exchange of ideas. *Boot camps* are workshops on steroids—a lot happening in a short time. *Trainings* and *classes* speak for themselves.

Take all of that into consideration when you're planning your marketing because different words do have an impact on people.

Please, Sir, Can I Have More?

How would you like to speak your way into a nice big, hefty pay-raise at your job? Then you need to conquer stage fright and fear of public speaking and master the expert presentation skills I teach!

Why?

Because as you move up "the food chain" you will reach a point where your ability to speak to groups of people will become necessary or even mandatory. There are so many businesses and industries where this is 100% true. In order to really get ahead, you'll need to be able to comfortably and confidently make presentations, pitches, or otherwise speak to a room full of prospects, clients, or even the board of directors. Never forget that your coworkers will prefer to not speak to groups due to fear, so they'll never resent you moving up since you're doing what they're not willing to do.

There's no doubt about it: **If you want to get ahead in your career faster and easier, you need to talk your way to the top!**

"Don't Wanters"

When you hold your own seminars, the people who show up want to be there. But when you speak at another organizations, beware that some or all of the group may only be there because they're being required to be there. It could be an issue of getting re-licensing credits or ongoing educational requirements or due to regulatory compliance issues. Or it could be simply that the boss said they have to be there—or else.

I've spoken to rooms full of people that were not there by choice. They were there by force. Can you imagine having to get up in front of a hostile crowd like that?

This is where your funny stories and anecdotes are going to come in very handy. Humor can defuse a situation like that in no-time flat. Also, keep your demeanor light and remember to smile. Your positive attitude can be positively infectious.

I've received some of my highest rave reviews and most glowing testimonials from initially hostile groups. Keep your sense of humor and have a great attitude—and you will too!

Scared?

Is there any difference between stage fright and fear of public speaking? How about performance anxiety? Does it matter?

There is a subtle but definite difference between stage fright and fear of public speaking. Stage fright is the fear or panic or freeze-up that can happen to people when they're on stage and in front of an audience. Fear of public speaking is a generalized fear of getting up in front of people—fear and terror that hits without even being in front of a group—for example, the night before a seminar talk. Performance anxiety also fits in this category.

Why is this distinction important? Because there are very different strategies for handling stage fright versus fear of public speaking. You'll want to use the right strategy for each, and of course, I'm providing you with a number of strategies and tactics to conquer stage fright and overcome fear of public speaking forever!

I'll Buy That Reason for $1

Are they buying your reasons or are you buying their excuses? There are many purposes to doing seminar speaking. You may be raising money for charity. You may be raising people's awareness about an important issue. You may be promoting and selling your products or services. You may be furthering a political candidacy. You may be training or educating people.

No matter what your purpose is, one thing is for sure true: either they are buying your reasons to vote, believe, buy, learn, or take whatever action you want them to take, or you are buying their reasons for not taking that action, learning, buying, and so forth.

It's your job to use all your skill, charm, humor, expertise and ability to make sure you sway your group over to you. Don't buy into people's excuses. Make them buy into your reasons!

Keep It Catchy & Snappy

Have you come up with a catchy title for your seminar or your talk? Rookie speakers overlook how important it is to have a snappy and catchy title for their seminar or their talk. Rookie speakers tend to focus on the talk itself—and certainly your presentation is important—but no one will ever hear it unless they're hooked into going in the first place.

Think about it. When you read a newspaper or a magazine, you scan along and then suddenly a headline grabs your attention. That's what your seminar title needs to do to your target market. Include your niche market in the title—"How Dog Groomers Can..."—and throw in some buzz words that grab attention, like *secret, tips, reveal, hidden, incredible, money.* (You can contact me if you want a list of hot buzz words to choose from.)

Make sure your title is enticing and makes your market want to know more—"7 Ways Dog Groomers Can Double Their Income In 30 Days". Spend a lot of time on your title, it's that important. Run several versions by some trusted friends or family.

Remember, first impressions are important. Without a catchy title,people might not even give your terrific seminar a second look.

Toastmasters International

No, it's not a fraternal brotherhood of people who like to toast bread! It's actually an organization that helps people who want to become speakers. Now, of course, I'm not trying to create competition for **The American Seminar Academy**, but you might as well know about Toastmasters if you don't already.

Toastmasters International has clubs everywhere. If you want a very cheap way to get your feet wet, this can be a good option for you since you'll get to make presentations in front of small groups and they'll count the "*ummms*" and "*uhhs*" you say, and help you with nervous gestures and other things like that. They'll be very supportive.

A quick internet search will pull them up for you, or you can contact me if you want more information at *www. SeminarAcademy.com*.

Who Wrote the Book?

Should you write a book on your topic?

Unequivocally, indisputably, indubitably, **YES!!** Having a book separates you from your competition and brands you as an expert. People have respect for someone that put the time and effort into producing a book. It elevates you in their minds. After all, you "wrote the book" on your topic.

You don't have to worry about going through a publishing house, you can self-publish—and you should. Your book can be a collection of articles you've already written. Or you can dictate it into a digital recorder and have a school kid transcribe it for you so you have your manuscript. You don't have to have an ISBN (bar code) if you're just selling and distributing it at solely at your seminars and to your clients. You can submit copyright paperwork, but that's not actually necessary either, nor is submitting to Library of Congress, but you can if you want or if you're planning on selling it retail and/or to libraries. Submit your manuscript in digital form to a print on demand printer with some cover design (get another student looking to build a portfolio or pay a graphic designer) and *voila!* You are an author!

Ghost writers can be expensive, but there are people who'll take your outline and create a book if you check with online freelance services. If you need help, you can contact me via *www.SeminarAcademy.com* because I have resources to jump start and shortcut your book writing success.

Market Thyself with Articles

Most people don't like to have to go out and cold call to try to find new business. So when it comes to speaking engagements and seminar speaking gigs, often people are reluctant to make the phone calls and do the "face time" necessary to get their name out there. But no one will call you to book a speaking gig if they don't know you're available and on what topic.

A very easy way to solve this is to write articles on your chosen topic in a variety of publications. That means newspapers, trade magazines, online—anywhere and everywhere you can.

Getting your articles published is much easier than you might think. Just make contact—ask the person that answers the phone who you need to speak with to obtain article submission criteria.

Then, just write and submit your articles. In your article, you can give a subtle "plug" for your speaking by mentioning an interesting question that came up in one of your talks. And, in your bio at the end of the article, be sure to mention you are available for speaking invitations!

More, More, More

You can't not think about what you don't want to think about without first thinking about it.

Think about that statement. You may need to read it several times before it sinks in. Here's the point: it comes down to *focus*.

Where is your mental focus? When it comes to conquering stage fright and fear of public speaking, trying to make it less just does not work. Don't try to be less of what you don't want. Don't put your mental focus on "I want to be less nervous." Instead, put your focus on what you do want. Put your attention and mental energy on being calm and confident.

Think about it this way: if you go into a dark room and want the darkness to be gone so you can see, should you try to have less darkness? Should you grab a broom and try to sweep the darkness out of the room? Or should you focus on finding the light switch and turning on the light? In this metaphor, you don't need less darkness, you need more light.

So when it comes to conquering stage fright and fear of public speaking, you don't need less nervousness. Decide what you need more of and focus on how you can have more of that.

"Always Leave 'Em Wanting More"

Seminar speakers can take a tip from the world of show business. Performers know that you want to satisfy your audience, but you also want them to want more of you. Are you giving away too much in your talk?

Look over the content of your talk with any eye to how you can deliver on the promise that your seminar title makes, while still leaving your group wanting more. A very simple way to do this is to tell them what they need to do, but not how to do it. Or, don't reveal every aspect of how to do it, leave some how-to information hinted at but not explicitly stated.

Think of it like an appetizer: a before-meal appetizer is not supposed to fill you up—yes, you get to eat something, but it's designed to whet your appetite, not completely satisfy it.

Take a tip from show business and "always leave 'em wanting more!"

Better Than Singing in the Shower

I've always wanted to sing so badly. And you know what? I got my wish—I sing so badly! But seriously, even if you can't sing, you can always improve your voice. And humming is a great way to improve your voice and make it more dynamic.

All you do is simply hum, but you start low and raise the pitch to as high as your vocal range will allow, then lower the pitch to as low as you can go. Rest, then repeat. As you do this, you want to have your throat be as relaxed as possible, refrain from any straining. Also, concentrate your voice in the area of the front of your face (called "the mask" in singing terms) where you feel the vibration more around your lips and nasal area than your throat.

Start humming your way to better vocal ability starting right now!

Props

Should you use props of some sort in your seminar talk? *Props*, in this use of the word, are physical objects you could use that help illustrate a point you're trying to make. For example, I once attended a seminar where the speaker was talking about problem solving. He called small problems "guppies" and he called big problems "whales". He had a couple stuffed animals he used as props—one was a guppy and one was a whale. So when he was talking about strategies to solve minor problems, he grabbed the guppy and held it up. When he talked about tactics to handle major problems, he held up the whale. Those props helped him to make his points in a humorous and memorable way.

Are there props that can help you make your point in a memorable way?

A good rule of thumb is that the props should not overshadow your talk or your message. Think of it as icing on a cake: a nice light layer of icing is nice, but few people want to eat a bowl of icing.

Stage Fright Be Gone!

How would you like to eradicate stage fright and fear of public speaking and improve your seminar speaking skills, all at the same time?

First, think of someone that has the kind of skill or ability that you'd like to have, someone who in your estimation embodies qualities you'd like to have when doing seminar speaking. Select someone who, in your mind, would never be nervous or anxious about doing public speaking. We'll call that person your "hero".

Next, mark out two spots on the floor about six or seven feet apart with tape or a small piece of paper. Designate one spot as *spot #1*, where you'll be you. The other spot, *spot #2*, will be where you'll "become" the person you selected as your hero.

Start at spot #1 and out loud deliver a few lines or paragraphs from your seminar talk. Then, walk over to spot #2 and "become" your hero and deliver the exact same lines being exactly like your hero—your face, voice, and body being just like your hero. Then go back to spot #1 and repeat that.

At first it might feel a little awkward, but keep doing it and keep trying it because soon you'll start to notice a difference in how you feel in spot #1 versus #2. This technique is extremely powerful, so try it right now!

Realize the Power

"The world stands aside and makes way for those who know where they're going"—Author Unknown

The power of seminar speaking is practically unlimited. It's a tool you can use for the rest of your life. When you realize the power of public speaking and group events, you'll never see the world the same way ever again.

With seminar speaking you can do so much more than the average person who doesn't use the power of seminar speaking. You can raise awareness, raise money, further political aspirations, gather community support—not to mention promote your business and fatten your bank account. When the light bulb goes on and you realize the power of seminar speaking, suddenly doors open for you that you didn't even know existed. You are able to use the tool of seminar speaking to get where you want to go.

When you know where you're going, and you have the power of seminar speaking on your side, what you can accomplish, create, sell, and achieve is limited only to your imagination.

There's a First Time for Everything

Whenever we do something new or for the first time, it's normal to have slight trepidation since we're in unknown territory.

When you do you first seminar or two, you're not sure what to expect exactly. Let's face it, the unknown makes the average person a little unsure. The first time you ever tried to drive a car was very different than the 100th time you drove, right? After a measure of experience driving, you don't even think twice about jumping into the driver's seat and taking off for wherever you want to go.

When you do you first seminar or two, why not ask a couple of supportive, good friends to attend? Having those friendly, smiling faces in the group will make your first experience or two just that much easier. Like using training wheels when learning to ride a bicycle, soon you feel comfortable and you can take the training wheels off.

Soon, you won't need the support of your friends, you'll be in familiar, comfortable territory whenever you do seminar speaking.

Another benefit of bringing a few supportive friends to your first seminar or two is you'll fill out the room a bit as well!

What Are THEY Doing?

Can other speakers help you to be a better seminar speaker?

Indirectly, yes. It's very easy to attend seminars, then just sit there and make notes about what you like and don't like about their presentation style. You can pay attention to how they use their voice, how they use or don't use the stage space. You can make notes about how they started their talk and how it was ended. You can make notes about audience reaction. You can makes note of any interesting or powerful quotes they used. You can notice if they use humor, and if it worked. You could pay close attention to how they use their face and what kind of gestures they make. Make notes about how they dressed and any use of props or visuals they used. You can also reverse engineer how they put their talk together based on the flow of content and how they present it.

Seminars and speaking engagements are all around you and are going on all the time Why not let other speakers help you to improve your game?

Mental Rehearsal

For many years now, star athletes have been not only doing physical practice and training, but they've been doing mental training as well. A number of famous athletes credit their mental training for giving them the edge over other highly talented players or opponents. Star athletes use the power of mental rehearsal. They mentally rehearse success. They clearly visualize making that shot, basket, hit, or goal.

Take a tip from winning athletes and do some mental training for your seminar speaking success. Clearly visualize yourself as being wildly successful. Visualizing your success sets up a winning mind-set.

On the other hand, most people actually rehearse failure! They visualize everything going wrong and doing a terrible job. Don't do that!

Mental training is what separates the best athletes from the good athletes. If it's good enough for star athletes, it's good enough for you!

"We Have Met the Enemy, and He Is Us!"

Pogo said that quote and it relates to public speaking like this: ***At the very heart of stage fright and fear of public speaking is the fact that you are paying way too much attention to you!***

You're all wrapped up in everything about you. How will people respond to you, how will you handle questions, how does your hair look, what if you...and on and on. Simply put, when you take the focus off of yourself, stage fright and fear of public speaking disappear like morning dew in bright sunlight. In a very real sense, we are our own worst enemy. We create bogey men that don't exist. There is a huge difference between what you make up in your mind and the realities of seminar speaking. We really need to get out of our own way so that we can reap the many rewards that seminar speaking has to offer.

Stop focusing on yourself. Start focusing on your seminar attendees and giving them what they came for. Put your focus on the outside world and it's realities, and not the phantoms that exists only in your imagination!

"Everything Is a Presentation"

I said that quote. I actually say it a *lot*. If you really stop and think about it, everything you do is in one form or another making a presentation. If you go on a job interview, how you present yourself will determine whether you get hired or not. When you go out on a date, your date will be evaluating how you present yourself. At work, how you present your ideas or your work makes a big difference in how it is received and evaluated.

Everything is a presentation.

When you master the expert presentation skills I teach you, you elevate yourself. You have many more choices in how you present yourself, your ideas, your message. You have been making presentations your whole life without even realizing it!

When you realize that everything is a presentation and that you can be a master of presentation skills, it's like holding a treasure map to guide you to a pot of gold!

Mind Molder

Perception is reality. When it comes to seminar speaking, this is something you need to know about and watch out for. People's perceptions about what is true or not true is all that matters.

As a seminar speaker, you have the power to dispel misconceptions. You have the power to shape and influence people's perceptions.

Now, I'm not saying that just because you get up and speak that you're going to rearrange everyone's reality and that they're going to shift their beliefs to align with whatever you say. However, people do tend to see seminar speakers as the expert. If you're trying to influence the thinking of a group of people in your talk, as a seminar speaker you have a lot of leverage.

Just keep in mind that people will be coming to your seminar with a whole host of preconceived notions and expectations, and that to them, their perception is their reality!

When They Ask How Much, You Say...

At some point, someone will ask you what your speaking fee is. I know, I know—you think that will never happen because you're not a "professional speaker". However, as you're going along doing your seminar speaking, someone is going to refer you to an organization that wants to pay you to speak on your topic.

When that happens—and it will happen!—your answer must not be "um...uh...I'll get back to you on that." No. You must be able to give them a quote right then and there. Your fee should vary depending on how long they want you to speak, so that's your first question when they ask about your fee. If you're actually going to be training and/or teaching, I suggest that your fee is also based on how many students you'll be training as well as the length of time. You should have an hourly rate, a half-day rate, and a daily rate ready to quote to anyone who asks about your speaking fee.

Even if you think you'll never get asked to speak for a fee, set up your rates ahead of time anyway—you may be surprised when someone does ask you, but at least you won't be unprepared!

A Hired Gun

Everything you've been told about how to conquer stage fright and fear of public speaking is wrong. Junk advice like "picture your audience naked" and "breathe deeply" just does not work. I teach you a number of ways to completely conquer stage fright that really do work. Stage fright is completely gone forever.

Very rarely, though, I get that one person in a million that just does not want to get up and speak—but they don't want to miss out on the huge benefits of seminar speaking.

So what's the answer? Simple: *Get someone else to speak instead of you.*

You do everything else. You handle the logistics, set up the presentation structure, and handle all the various details getting the seminar set up. Then, you sit back and relax while your "hired gun" does the actual presenting and speaking. Easy cure, eh? There are countless speakers you can get for free or very cheap. Contact me if you need help with that.

Ask anyone who used to be afraid of public speaking, and they'll tell you that now they're addicted and it's fun! But if you just will not do it no matter what, you can still reap the many benefits of seminars by bringing in someone to speak on your behalf.

Ridin' the Coattails

Ready for another easy way to find seminars where you can speak and promote your business, and sell your product or service?

The easiest way to get a room full of people, is to speak at a seminar someone else has put together. They've gotten the "butts in the seats" and you don't have to bother with marketing, which can be expensive.

Here's another great way to take advantage of existing seminars: look in trade magazines for seminars that are being promoted. Don't contact the promoter and tell them your fee. Instead, tell them you'll speak for free. That will get their attention for sure. If you really want to get their attention, tell them that you want to pay them to speak! How? By giving them a split on revenues generated by your talk! If you have a product or service to sell, sign people up right there at the seminar, and give the promoter a split—50% ought to get their attention.

Using this approach means the seminar promoter has nothing to lose. You're going to provide a valuable seminar talk and it costs him or her absolutely nothing. Plus, they stand to make money by having you there!

Like Bees to Honey

Your seminar will have a lot of appeal when you dress it up as a social occasion. People are used to going to seminars in hotel meeting and banquet rooms. But if you choose a venue like an upscale restaurant or a country club, you can create an aura of a classy social occasion. You will give the ladies a great reason to put on a nice dress, some jewelry, and their favorite perfume. The men will get to look good next to their ladies, look dapper themselves, and rub elbows with the rest of the sophisticates who will ostensibly be there. Resistance is low to going to a nice restaurant or checking out the country club if they're not already a member.

Your seminar promotion should be in the style of a classy wedding invitation. At the seminar, treat the event like a social occasion—that just happens to have you making a presentation on your topic.

Use this in conjunction with other techniques I teach you like door prizes and grand prize drawings to really make your seminar a must-attend event, and people will be lining up to get in!

Should I Stay or Should I Go?

What should you do after your seminar? There are some who say you should completely disappear after you've done your seminar talk. There are merits to this, not the least of which is the mystique you create and the fact that you don't have to drain yourself with endless questions after you've given your all onstage.

However, I'm of the opinion that you should stick around and talk to people after you speak. I've done it both ways, and my experience is that you'll create more of a connection with people when you hang out with them afterward.

However, a word of caution is in order here: sometimes there is a person or persons that want to "pick your brain" but what they really want to do is "suck you dry" for all your expertise and information. These people will not do business with you—they're trying to get it out of you for free.

Also, as a group may form around you, be sure to give everyone a chance to ask their question and don't let any one person capitalize on your time and attention.

It's up to you whether you stay around after your seminar talk or not, try it both ways and see which works best for you.

It's Not What They Say...

It's only natural for us to enjoy a positive response from an audience. When people in your seminar are nodding, smiling, and clapping, it's totally normal and natural that a positive response like that would make you feel good. But the opposite is not necessarily true.

In other words, if they're *not* smiling, nodding and clapping, that does *not* mean you're doing a bad job! I've done literally thousands of workshops, seminars, trainings, classes, speeches, and other group events and I can say without a doubt that *audience response is not a reliable measure of your success.*

Resist the almost overwhelming temptation to want to see obvious signs of approval and liking from your audience. Yes, those signs of approval feel good, but don't use them as a measure of success. Instead, use "hard numbers" to evaluate your success—hard numbers like total sales, total number of appointments made, total donation dollars pledged, total signatures obtained on a petition, and so forth.

Audience approval feels good, but it's not a good measure of seminar success. Stay focused on the goals you're trying to achieve with your seminar speaking, and use hard numbers to evaluate your success.

Let's Take Ten

How often should you schedule breaks during your seminar talk?

If you conduct a seminar talk longer than an hour and a half, you're going to have to give people a break, if for no other reason than to allow your group a chance to go to the bathroom. People also need a chance to stretch, and many times the seats won't be particularly comfortable, so you're going to need to give people's butts a break, too! People will have a hard time listening to your well-planned, superbly structured, expertly presented seminar talk when all they can think about is that they've lost all feeling in their lower body.

A good rule of thumb is to give people a break every 1½ hours. Every hour is too often, and two hours is pushing the limits of tolerance.

Of course, taking breaks also means you have the problems of losing momentum and also getting everyone back into their seats in a timely manner. To counter this problem, do a "cliff hanger" and entice them with some juicy info you'll share after the break.

Always remember, the brain will not absorb what the butt cannot endure! So, be kind to both and give them a break.

A Vodka Martini, Shaken Not Stirred

Should you agree to a seminar speaking engagement if you're scheduled to speak after a cocktail hour?

The beauty of holding your own seminars—or at least being the organizer if you're not the main presenter—is that you control the timing and flow. But if you're going to be a guest speaker at someone else's seminar, you don't have that luxury. If you're one of a number of speakers during a day-long event that runs into the evening, you could potentially get stuck with the after-cocktail-hour slot.

If people have been drinking, their inhibitions drop and you're much more likely to have to put up with heckling and possibly even outright rude or even hostile behavior. If you think you can handle that, then that's fine, but you will always want to ask the organizer exactly what your time-slot is to speak.

If you know up front you'll be the after-cocktails speaker, then at least you can be prepared. And, if you're particularly funny, that time-slot could even be to your advantage!

Arizona or Alaska?

No, the question here is not what state should you hold your seminar in. This tip has to do with the climate in the room where you'll be speaking. Many seminars are held in rooms that have a climate control system, such as hotel banquet and meeting rooms with central air conditioning, or, in smaller rooms, sometimes it's an air conditioning unit. It seems that the room is always either too hot or too cold. It's rare to get that "just perfect" temperature setting—when the air kicks on, it gets too cold, then after it kicks off, it gets too hot. First Alaska, then Arizona.

You can't spend a lot of your time worrying about this, you'll just have to go with the flow. Set the room temperature before your group arrives and remember that they're going to generate heat, so you typically want to set it a little colder than you might if you were in the room alone. 68-70 degrees is a common rule of thumb.

Forget about trying to make it perfect for everyone, because there will always be someone freezing because they're sitting right under the vent, and everyone else is comfortable. Just set it the best you can and leave it, unless everyone agrees it's Arizona or Alaska.

FAQ

When you hear the same questions repeated in various seminar talks you do, this is something you want to perk up and pay attention to.

First of all, what is the nature of this question? Is the question about how to do something, or a "what" question about facts or data? Is it a "why" question about the purpose of something?

Stop and carefully consider the nature of the question and why people ask that question in particular. Now, incorporate the answer to this question into your actual seminar talk. In other words, you're solving the problem in people's minds ahead of time. Even if the question is not actually about a problem, you're doing everyone a good service by bringing up the common questions you get ahead of time, and answering them during your talk.

The common questions people ask are an important asset to you, and you should always pay close attention to them—the answers to those questions are going to be what helps you gain business!

"Hit the Road, Jack!"

Depending on your business and your purpose for doing Seminar Speaking, you could end up needing or wanting to speak outside of your hometown or business trading area. If that becomes true for you, you're going to need to be prepared for life on the road.

Although it might seem glamorous from the outside, life on the road can be difficult and draining. Now, some people take to life on the road better than others. For some, it's an exciting adventure that they never tire of, while for others it's an exhausting ordeal.

Plan for your comfort. Take snacks you enjoy, ear plugs for noisy hotel rooms so you can sleep, and some reading and listening material. Naturally, you can decide for yourself what helps to make your road adventure more enjoyable. If you can find some time to do a little sight-seeing and visit places of interest to you, that will also make your trip much more enjoyable.

Finally, be sure to make connections with people you meet on the road. They can be future allies, business contacts, and friends.

The Round Table

When you do your seminar, for the most part it's you up there talking and sharing your knowledge with your audience. In other words, while there may be some give and take between you and your group, you'll be doing the majority of the talking. But, you can extend extra value to your group by offering a separate "round table discussion" after your seminar.

The round table event can follow your seminar, or it can be scheduled for a separate date. Usually, your attendance will be better if it follows the seminar because people are already there. You can charge extra for this round table discussion where you'll provide exclusive consulting for this smaller group, or you can limit participation only to those who purchase your product or service offered at the seminar, or who book appointments with you.

People love to be "in" on an exclusive event, so it's best if you position your bonus round table discussion as being limited only to those who've met certain conditions you've predefined.

Tele-Seminars

When we think of seminar speaking, we usually mean a room where you stand up in front of people who have assembled to hear your presentation. Did you know you can do the same thing on the phone?

You can, and you should! It's called a *tele-seminar*, and you do your entire seminar never leaving the comfort of your home or office. You could be at home, in your comfy clothes, with a cup of tea and your feet up delivering your terrific presentation. And, your participants don't have to leave home either. This is particularly helpful if they don't live within driving distance of your usual seminar location. In your tele-seminar, you can even control and monitor much of the event online via websites that offer teleconferencing—and for free!

I've held quite a number of successful tele-seminars, and so can you. Feel free to contact me via *www.SeminarAcademy.com* and I'll tell you which is my current favorite free teleconferencing website.

It's Not Bragging If It's True

Quite a number of years ago, I was in charge of organizing seminars for a group of chiropractors. We held special dinner seminars for existing patients who would invite friends and family to join. The doctors had a number of letters patients had written thanking them for their dramatic improvements in health, how they were no longer suffering pain, and so forth. The doctors had obtained permission to share those letters, and they would read them aloud near the end of the seminar. Those testimonial letters always had a very strong effect on the audience. After the seminar, the friends and family all wanted to book appointments to see the doctors for their pains and problems. And, every once in a while, one of the patients at our dinner seminars would interrupt and ask for permission to share their story of how the doctors had gotten them out of pain and able to live a normal life again.

You may not be a doctor, but your clients' success stories are a very powerful tool to help your prospects become your clients!

Values Elicitation

Here's a very valuable little exercise that can really help you to clarify your purpose and what's important to you. Some call this a **values elicitation** because you are uncovering precisely what is most important to you in a specific context.

In fact, values are the answer to the question, *What's important to you about _____* (fill in the blank). Beliefs and values are closely linked, but values are usually below the level of our conscious awareness. When I've done values elicitations with clients, the most common response is a degree of surprise or even shock at uncovering what turns out to be most important in some area.

Uncover your top five values in the context of your business, and in doing seminars simply by asking yourself *What's important to me about that?* and then quickly jotting down everything you can think of. Finally, pick out the top five in order of importance, with the first being most important.

This is an extremely powerful exercise because our top five values are typically what generate our behaviors. Take the time to uncover your top five values right now!

Now and Later

Should you allow seminar attendees to attend your future seminars at a discount or even for free? This is a terrific way to create a lot of extra value for your paid seminar attendees and doesn't really cost you anything.

As part of your seminar promotion for your paid seminars, you can mention this benefit of attending. People see a lot of value in being able to attend your future seminars for free or at a discount. There's a lot of flexibility in how you structure this, and here's a few examples to stimulate your thinking.

One example is to allow people to attend this same seminar offering in the future for free. Or it can be free but limited to the next year or 2 years. Another great variation is to allow them to attend future seminars for half price. All of these variations are on the same seminar offering, but you can also extend discount offers to different seminars you offer as well.

If you want you can give them a club membership certificate that entitles them to the various future benefits you offer. Everyone likes to get a great deal and feel part of an exclusive group!

Tell Your Friends

It's often true that even people who are extremely satisfied with your products or services forget to refer people to you. You can give them a gentle reminder that you appreciate their referrals by passing out cards that have spaces for them to write down their referrals for you to follow up on. Word of mouth is an extremely strong marketing method, and passing out referral cards can take many variations.

You can request they write down the names and contact info of 3 or 5 people they believe would benefit from what you do. Or you can pass out special referral cards for your satisfied clients to give to people, and those referral cards can be in the form of a gift certificate or discount coupon.

Whatever form your referral cards, coupons, or gift certificates take, the point is to remind your satisfied clients and customers that you appreciate their referrals.

Step by Step

Do you have a product, service, or seminar ladder?

A **product, service or seminar ladder** is where you have a series of offerings at different price points.

The idea is that you have at least one or two low cost items that allow people to "test the waters" without making a large financial investment. Then you have price points that are higher and higher, all the way up to your most expensive offering.

Having a product, service, or seminar ladder doesn't mean that people will always start at the bottom with the lowest priced item, then work their way up, but that can happen.

Some people will start at the top of the ladder because many believe that price equals quality. In that instance, they won't be interested in the lower priced items because they'll see them as not having the quality of the higher priced items.

Having a ladder of products, services and seminars means people can enter at whatever price point level that is most comfortable and appealing to them.

Ask the Expert

When you do seminar speaking, it brands you as an expert. When you hold regular seminars, people start to see you as almost an institution in your area. Even people that never attend your seminar will see you as the local community expert. People will want to do business with you when they see you as the expert in the local community in your chosen field and business or industry. What's more, people will actually refer their friends and family to you, even if they've never done business with you. Why? Because you're the local expert!

Doing just one or two seminars is not enough. To become the local community expert you're going to have to hold seminars on a regular basis, and pretty soon you'll start to see the benefits of your efforts paying off as you become almost a celebrity!

The Entertainment Factor

I've never thought of myself as particularly funny, and when I started doing seminars, I didn't have any jokes planned or any funny stories to tell. However, I found the group would start laughing out loud periodically during my seminar. Then at my second seminar, the same thing happened. I was actually quite surprised to discover that I was naturally funny.

I had never planned to be funny, but I found that during the course of my talk, I had funny things to say and would make funny observations. You might find the same thing happens to you. In fact, it's quite possible you might discover all kinds of talents you have that you never knew existed! It really doesn't matter if you do or not, the bottom line is to do your seminar speaking and stay focused on your purpose.

But, don't be at all surprised if you're much more entertaining than you ever gave yourself credit for!

Never Hesitate to Invest in Yourself

I'm a little embarrassed to admit that I've had to learn this lesson the hard way. I remember there was a training I wanted to attend and they also had a product I wanted to purchase. I really had a feeling that this training and product would make a huge difference in my business. For a year, I thought about it and tried to convince myself that I probably already knew everything that I would learn in the seminar and product.

Finally, after a year, I gritted my teeth and I made the purchases.

It was one of the best decisions of my life! It filled in the missing pieces I needed so badly. If I had simply invested in that training and product the year before when I was thinking about it, I would have been much, much further along in my business.

The moral of the story is **never hesitate to invest in yourself.** Be sure to go to *www.SeminarAcademy.com* and see which of my seminars and products are going to take you to the next level!

Gimmicks

Should you have some kind of gimmick when you do your seminar speaking?

I once knew a financial planner who would start his seminars by coming out in a gorilla suit. The somewhat stunned and definitely curious crowd would be drop-jawed waiting to see what would happen next. He would take off the gorilla head, shake his head, then say, "Boy, it's really a jungle out there!" and people would howl with laughter—most of the time. Other times it would completely bomb. But, for sure he grabbed people's attention, and for sure they remembered him.

Having a gimmick is highly questionable—this is something that if you can make it work, it will really work well, but you really run a risk of it not working at all.

Finally, the positives of having a gimmick need to be weighed out against the negatives—will people take you and your business seriously if you come out in a gorilla suit?

Think about the message you are trying to convey and your audience, then decide if a gimmick would work for you.

You and Trade Shows

Something that can definitely help out your seminar speaking is to attend trade shows in your area of interest.

First, industry trade shows will typically showcase the latest developments in the field. You can gain a wealth of knowledge about what's hot and what's happening.

Second, you can make a lot of contacts. The typical trade show will be packed with booths staffed by friendly people who are more than glad to chat with you at length. Be sure to take a small notepad or voice recorder to capture the main points you want to remember after your chats.

Also, you can pick up a giant amount of free literature that can give you tons of ideas about what to add to your seminars.

You can also keep up on what the competition is doing so you're never in the dark about their latest offerings.

Lastly, trade shows are also a lot of fun, which is just icing on the cake!

Your Voice: Care and Upkeep

I have very rarely lost my voice due to over-use. There are probably some friends and relatives who wish I'd lose my voice, but that's a whole different story.

As a seasoned professional seminar speaker, I want to introduce you to a tea you must know about—even if you're not much of a tea drinker. I strongly suggest that you pick up some tea that is make of the herb *slippery elm bark*. This tea has no caffeine, and has a very pleasant taste requiring no sweeteners. A hot drink will open up your throat, and the slippery elm bark coats and soothes it.

Avoid cold drinks since they tend to constrict your throat. Water at room temperature is best. Believe it or not, eating french fries within an hour before you have a talk has a remarkably soothing effect on your voice as well!

Taking care of your voice is pretty easy when you follow a few simple rules, and if you take good care of your voice, your voice will take good care of you.

Everywhere a School

You can learn quite a lot by attending seminars and absorbing everything you see and hear, but don't discount the value of what you can incorporate into your seminars in places that have absolutely nothing to do with seminars. For example, you may overhear a great quote in conversations that you can use, or a terrific story that fits right into what you do. You may be reading a book or watching a movie that gives you new ideas you can incorporate. You could be watching TV and suddenly be struck by something that would be perfect in your seminar talk. Even music can inspire you or give you new ideas you can use in your seminar talk.

Just by opening your mind, you can find inspiration and ideas almost anywhere that will enhance your seminar talks.

Give 'Em a Lil' Somethin' Somethin'

What are you giving out at your seminars?

In this case I'm talking about the materials you distribute to your seminar attendees. This is something you can adjust and change over time, but you'll want to think ahead about what kind of items you're going to give to the people who attend your seminar talks. For example, are you going to give them brochures to take home to peruse later? How about price sheets? Do you have literature that would benefit your groups? Audio CD's they should listen to? DVD's they should watch?

People that attend your seminars are going to want to take something with them that allows them to review what you presented, do more research, and reflect on the information you talked about in your seminar. Make it easy on them and be sure to give them materials to take with them.

Look at the Benefits

Here's an exercise that will prove of great value to you in your seminar speaking,

Take out two pieces of paper. At the top of one, write the word "*features*" and on the other write the word "*benefits*".

Start with the *features* page and begin to write down words and short phrases about what's great about your product, your service, your business. Write down everything you can think of that's special about what you do.

Now, on the other page titled *benefits*, write down words and short phrases that describe exactly how your product, service, business benefits people. What do they get? How does their life improve? On your benefits page, also include all the things that people will lose if they don't use your product, service, or business.

Most people primarily emphasize features in their seminar speaking. I'd like to suggest you lean more heavily toward emphasizing benefits, and you'll get better results.

What Was That in the Middle?

Did you know that people tend to mostly recall the first and last things they hear? Psychologists have done research on this and in my experience this is really true. People do seem to mostly recall your "opener" and your "closer", with most of the emphasis on your closer, which is the last thing you say.

You should prepare several different openers and closers. Shoot for creating openers that are funny, shocking, and create a lot of interest in what will follow. Also create a number of closers that leave your group with what you most want them to remember later. Another way to think about closers is what state of mind or emotional state do you want your group to be in at the end of your seminar?

Preparing several openers and closers gives you choice and flexibility because you can deliver your basic seminar talk, but alternate openers and closers depending on the mood of the group and your needs and wants at the moment.

Just Do It

When it comes to seminar speaking, you're going to have to make contact with a number of people. Many times you'll find yourself in a position where you need to contact an organization where you may be able to conduct a seminar. In that situation, you may find yourself hesitating. In those moments of hesitation, you might question whether the person on the other end of the phone will be receptive to your call, or resistant. Many times, this is where people decide not to take action and don't pick up the phone.

This has happened to me a number of times, and I've always been surprised at how the phone call actually turns out differently from what I expected. Often we create scenarios in our minds that are just not reality. Don't talk yourself out of making calls, just make the calls and see what actually happens.

Don't decide for others what their response will or won't be. When it comes to making the calls, don't think about it, just do it!

Define Your Success

How do you define seminar success? Is it in sales dollars? Standing ovations? People that tell you that you're great? Is it in money raised for charity? Petition signatures? Smiles on people's faces?

Clearly, you can define your seminar success however you wish. Whichever way you define it, *I highly suggest you define it!* Many people don't and if you ask them if their seminar was a success, you'll get "I guess so..."

Define your goal(s) for your seminar, then measure your success against that. Goals can be hard or soft. Hard goals include amount of money brought in, appointments made, number of signatures on a petition. Soft goals are audience enjoyment, client satisfaction, how you feel about how things went. In other words, soft goals are intangible, hard goals are tangible.

Decide what seminar success means to you. Define it, then measure it. Keep records of your successes so you can track your improvement over time.

Someone's Already Doing It!

People often become discouraged if their research indicates they face a lot of competitors in the marketplace. However, the reality is that if you look around and see tons of competition, you should jump for joy!

No, I haven't gone crazy. The reason why you should celebrate lots of competition is because it means you are in a fertile market. If you look around and see very little or even no competition in a market, you should be concerned. Why? Because there are truly very few new ideas out there. If there's no competition, it's pretty likely that there's also no demand. Sure, it's possible you've "invented the wheel" and discovered a completely untapped market, but it's also not very likely either.

Having lots of competition simply means you only need to figure out how to carve out your share of an existing market of hungry buyers. The demand is already there, you just need to be one of the suppliers.

The Gaps

When you research your competition, you may find that you can do a better job of delivering your product or service than your competitors do. Or you may discover that there is a need that the market demands but is not being fulfilled by the competition.

Look closely at what and how your competition is operating in the marketplace. Carefully compare that with your surveys and research into what buyers in the marketplace want. Figure out what buyers want that is not being delivered by your competition—either not being delivered at all or not in sufficient supply. Examples of gaps you could fill in the marketplace include high levels of personal attention, better customer service, faster or cheaper product or service delivery, or better follow-through after the sale has been made.

Once you've listed up the ways you can fill needs in the marketplace that your competition is not, be sure to communicate that clearly in all of your seminar speaking.

Co-opetition

Co-opetition is a term recently coined that is a fusion of two words: *cooperation* and *competition*. In brief, it means cooperating with your competition. No, I'm not talking about price fixing or other such practices. Co-opetition means you create joint ventures for mutual profitability.

Sure, there are some cases or industries where the last thing you'd ever want to do is cooperate with the competition. I understand that. But, very often people misjudge competition and see it as something to be conquered or banished and they completely miss out on the fact that with a little creative thinking, you could actually benefit each other.

There's an old German story about two sisters that kill each other over an orange, and it turns out that one sister only wanted the orange peel to bake with and the other wanted the orange meat to eat! If they'd each known the desire of the other, they could have each gotten exactly what they wanted.

You may not be able to make co-opetition work for you in your area or industry, but if you've never considered it before, start thinking creatively about how to make co-opetition work for you.

The World's Greatest

There's a guy who's been selling big-screen TV's here in the Los Angeles area for years and calls himself "The King of Big Screen". He comes on at the end of a TV spot and says "I AM the king!" and he's wearing a robe and a crown. It's kind of silly, but it's also highly memorable. In practically every town there's some guy who's "Crazy Eddie" or whatever his name is, and he's crazy because his prices are so low, he must be insane.

Now, in your industry, business, or profession it might not be appropriate to have a title like "The Queen of Real Estate" or "The Love Doctor" or "The Money Mechanic", but on the other hand a catchy and memorable title might be just the thing to help separate you out from the rest of the competition in your area. Claiming a title can be a clever way to stand out from the crowd and be more memorable to your target market.

If you did claim a title, what would it be?

If you do end up claiming a title, you can certainly use that in your introduction at your seminars—and in your marketing.

Show 'Em How It's Done

Demonstrations can be a terrific convincer and convert skeptics into believers. For example, alternative health practitioners have done demos where they measurably reduce stiffness or pain in someone in the group. That's pretty common. Another situation where demos are used in seminars are when the seminar is teaching some kind of skill or technique and someone from the group is brought up front, taught that specific skill or technique, and right in front of everyone masters that skill, or at least displays competency. That kind of demo can create confidence in the rest of the group that they can also be competent as well.

The real goal of any demonstration you do in your seminars boils down to the rest of the group thinking to themselves either "I want that" or "I can do that too".

The Value of Handouts

Handouts are materials that support your actual presentation. In this case, the word "handouts" does *not* refer to your brochures, price sheets, or other free informational and/or promotional materials you give people to take home with them. In this case handouts refers to materials supporting your presentation, such as an outline of your seminar talk.

I've given out many variations of handouts—everything from a summary outline of my seminar, all the way up to virtually a transcript of everything I covered. I've also experimented with giving out no handouts whatsoever. People see value in handouts, but few of them will really get them out later and look them over. In most cases, the handouts will get filed away somewhere never to be seen again, or just tossed in the trash.

If you are going to have handouts that follow your presentation so that people can take notes, I suggest you make it just a bare outline and not a detailed outline of your seminar talk. If you're using a PowerPoint Presentation, then it's easy to create handouts by using the print function.

Handouts may or may not be necessary depending on the topic and goals of your seminar, but you should try it both ways to see whether handouts make your seminars more successful, or make no difference.

Is It a Distraction?

Handouts can add to your seminar or they can take away from it. Handouts can add to your seminar when they provide space for people to take notes. Handouts also add to your seminar when they contain your contact info—that is, if you are interested in having people contact you. Handouts can add to your seminar when they also "just happen" to include promotional material for your products and services. And, handouts can add to your seminar when they offer additional perceived value to your attendees.

But, handouts take away from your seminar when people read ahead and already know what you're going to say. Handouts take away from your seminar especially when people's focus is on the handouts—and not on you. Handouts also take away from your seminar if all they do is cost you money, and then people throw them away afterwards.

You can decide ahead of time whether you'll include handouts or not. Just remember that there's no substitute for testing and then evaluating the results over time.

Location, Location, Location

There's an old saying about getting rich in real estate—you only need to consider three things: location, location, location.

In the seminar speaking business, location can make a huge difference—and in this case I'm not talking about if you're holding your seminar in a hotel or your office. I'm talking about what city you hold your seminar in. In the U.S., most of the major cities are major draws. New York, Los Angeles, Miami, Atlantic City and Los Vegas are very popular locations.

Other major draws include resort locations such as Hawaii, Fiji, Acapulco, and other desirable vacation destinations.

Holding your seminar in desirable locations gives people the chance to not only attend your seminar, but to also get in a vacation at the same time. Plus, if it's a business expense, your attendees may also be able to write off a portion of the expenses on their taxes.

Consider if your seminar event might benefit by being held in a resort or desirable destination location.

The Write Stuff

Should you write a book on your topic or area of expertise?

Yes, you should. But before you roll your eyes and say that it's too much work or impossible for you, having your own book is well within your reach.

First, take a relieving deep breath and realize you don't have to lock yourself in a room for months on end and try to create some kind of masterpiece.

Pick an aspect of your topic that you're most passionate about. Create an outline—use the "tell 'em, tell 'em, tell 'em" format I teach you. That's your skeleton. Now just put the flesh on it by filling out the details. Once you're done, you can review and add additional information. Don't get lost in rewriting, just get it done. You don't have to worry about getting a publisher or ISBN number unless you're planning to try to retail your book. If you need help, I can help you with various aspects of getting your book done.

Writing a book positions you as an expert, and you are an expert at what you do. So get started right now and get your book done!

Beware Super Bowl Sunday!

Attendance at your seminars can be strongly affected by events such as holidays and sporting events. When planning to hold a seminar, you need to stop and consider if there are any holidays or sports events that might negatively affect your seminar attendance. It might seem obvious to you that you need to be mindful of these types of events, but in practice people often completely forget to stop and think about it at all when they do their seminar scheduling.

Holidays and sports events are not the only events you have to watch out for so be sure to stop and carefully consider what might affect attendance at your seminar.

Piggybacking

A clever seminar scheduling strategy can be to hold what's called a *piggyback seminar*. This is where you hold a seminar in the same venue either right before or right after another seminar on your same topic was held. For example, if there will be an industry convention held with a large amount of attendees, you can hold your seminar right after the big convention and you stand a very good chance of getting a good number of people who'll want to attend your seminar too. You can do the same thing by holding your seminar before the industry convention.

Come up with a unique angle on the convention topic, or even a controversial slant, and people will be intrigued and curious.

There's absolutely nothing wrong with piggybacking onto industry events and conventions, so take advantage of this clever way of scheduling your seminar!

A Little Warning

How much lead time should you budget between when you start promoting your seminar, and the actual date of the seminar?

Start your seminar promotions too far in advance, and people will completely forget the event was ever booked. Start promoting too late, and you don't give people enough time to make plans to attend. If you tell people about an event that is months away, psychologically they'll tune it out because it's too far out for them to take it seriously yet. If its days away, they may already have a full calendar and can't make it even if they want to. If you're doing a multi-day training, give people more time to prepare since they'll have to think about blocking out time, reserving accommodations, and so forth. If you're doing a short introductory evening, you don't need nearly as much lead time.

A general rule of thumb is to start your serious promotions about six weeks in advance of your actual seminar date.

You? Funny and Inspiring?

How is it possible to be inspiring or funny, when you're not particularly inspiring and you're not naturally funny?

This is where you want to have a file full of inspiring quotes and stories *and* a file full of funny quotes and stories. Then, when your preparing to do a seminar talk, all you have to do is reach into your file full of inspiring and funny quotes and stories, and pick which one is appropriate for that seminar.

Now, I've already done the work for you because in my home study course for Seminar Speaking Success, I've included books full of funny and inspiring stories and quotes! You can get more info at *www.SeminarAcademy.com*, or by contacting me directly via that website. Either that or just be sure to collect quotes and stories that and inspiring and funny. They're all around you!

Not everyone is inspiring and not everyone is funny—but that doesn't matter. All you need are the quotes and stories and you're now inspiring and funny.

Stay on Target

When you deliver your seminar, are you doing it *on purpose*? In this case, when I say "on purpose" I don't mean "deliberately". What I mean is, *are you focused on your purpose?*

This is something that people easily lose sight of when planning and even when delivering their seminar. You simply must stay "on purpose", meaning you must never lose sight of the reason(s) you're doing your seminar speaking in general, and this particular seminar you're doing or are about to do. If your seminar is designed to get people to make an appointment, never forget that. If your seminar is to raise money or awareness, keep that firmly in your mind. If your seminar is to educate or train, stay focused on that task. If your seminar is to sell your product or service, make sure you never lose sight of that.

Staying "on-purpose" is absolutely vital to your seminar success!

Bonus Tip:
Rocky Had Mickey...
Who's in Your Corner?

I'm certain that you know the plot of the movie *Rocky*: Rocky is a down-on-his-luck fighter who gets the chance to box the world Champion, Apollo Creed. Rocky trains for the fight alone until Mickey comes to coach and train him. With the help of Mickey, Rocky holds his own again the champion and emerges victorious.

Every public speaker possesses natural talent and learned skill. But, who is in your corner to help you hone that talent and skill so that you become, in the words of Mickey, "a very dangerous person", meaning that you are the best that you can be?

Like Rocky as he trained for the big bout, as you conduct seminars and speak in public, you will inevitably encounter obstacles along the way. Some you will overcome as if they weren't even there while others will try to stop you like a "solid right" to the jaw.

For some, a major issue is stage fright and fear of public speaking. It's a shame, because that is so easily conquered. You should not let such a small issue stand between you and your success. I realize that stage fright may seem like a big scary monster, but every single person who conquers it looks back and laughs at the idea that they were ever afraid of public speaking.

Probably one of the biggest barriers to holding seminars—right after stage fright and fear of public speaking—is the mistaken idea people have about answering questions when they're doing public speaking and seminars. Their fear is that they'll be asked a question they either don't know the answer to or just don't know how to handle. Like fear of public speaking, this is a very understandable fear—until you discover that there are many easily-learned and quickly-mastered strategies for handling even the most difficult and challenging questions (or even bizarre or irrelevant questions!) and easily handling questions you don't know the answer to. Your fear quickly evaporates when you are armed with techniques for handling *any* question that could come your way.

Another barrier that stops many people from achieving their goals with speaking and seminars is that they've heard that to be successful with seminars, they have to be funny—and they don't believe they are funny. This is something that is so very easy to solve that I'm quite shocked that anyone lets such a trifling matter stop them from putting huge amounts of money in the bank, improving their lifestyle, and providing more for themselves and the ones that they love. It's absolutely *not* required for you to be funny in order to achieve the desired results with your speaking and seminars. No one should ever let "I'm not funny" stand in the way of their success.

Similarly, there are a certain percentage of people who believe they must be able to inspire and uplift a crowd in order to achieve success with seminars. Just like being funny, being inspirational is certainly not a pre-requisite to seminar success.

One of the other major obstacles I find that stops people from enjoying all the income and success that speaking and seminars bring is that they're not quite sure how to properly structure an effective seminar presentation. This is a very real problem in that many times business owners think they should just get up and talk about their product or service, or educate the group about some aspect of their field of expertise, but this is a *huge* mistake. Research studies and my own direct experience conclusively shows that that informing or educating simply does *not* convert prospects into customers in a speaking or seminar setting. Many business owners are out there right now doing seminars with the deadly mistaken idea that they can get up in front of people and simply educate or inform them into becoming paying customers. Those business owners are wasting their time and money because even if they do get some meager results from those seminars, with some minor adjustments to their presentation structure, they can greatly increase their conversion rate and get dramatically better results.

Some people have tried doing a seminar or three or more in the past, but they got poor or no results, and so they conclude that seminars "don't work." This is as ridiculous as trying to ride a bicycle for the first time, failing at it, then concluding that "bicycles don't work." Ludicrous! Unfortunately, those people sometimes become so narrowly focused on those past failures that they're afraid to even try again. That is truly a shame because they deprive themselves of the single best method of marketing that ever existed and ever will exist.

All of these obstacles have one thing in common: **They deprive people of the major ongoing benefits they would receive if only they took the time to get proper information and training on how to succeed with seminars and public speaking.**

Over the course of conducting 1,893 seminars, workshops, trainings and other group events, I look back and realize that I made a lot of mistakes. Over the years, I have been personally trained and coached by some of the best and most successful seminar speakers out there. I'm certain that the biggest mistake I made was not getting that information and training sooner. I wasted a lot of time and I forfeited a large amount of income. With 20-20 hindsight, I realize now that I should never have hesitated to get the high-level information and training that would have allowed me to reach my goals much sooner.

In short, if I had taken a "Mickey" into my corner sooner in my career, I wouldn't have had my "nose" broken so many times! There are indeed a number of nuances and inside tips to making seminars the kind of resounding success that makes a person's business grow to whatever level is desired.

That's why I write books like this and train people in the art of public speaking and seminars. That's why I formed the American Seminar Academy (*www.AmericanSeminarAcademy.com*). **For speakers everywhere, at every level of skill and talent, I work to improve those skills so that every speaker can become better, can become that "dangerous person", that speaker who accomplishes his goals and becomes a star in his or her field.**

The gains that my students and clients have made *far* exceed what they could have done if merely left on their own, like Rocky did with Mickey. Without Mickey, Rockey would probably have been KO'ed within the first few rounds; but because Mickey trained and guided him, he helped Rocky through all the obstacles and potential pitfalls and made a champion of him.

I cannot urge you enough to get someone in your corner, someone who knows the ropes of public speaking and seminars, someone who can take your skill and hone it to razor-sharpness, someone who wants you to succeed in a way that is even greater than you imagined. It doesn't have to be me, but make sure that you have a good trainer and "corner man."

With this book, I've set before you 129 powerful ways

that you can improve your seminars. Your first step to seminar speaking success is to use these tips and improve yourself. Your next step is to find a great trainer to coach you to excellence.

If you would like to contact me for information regarding the trainings that I do or other products that I have that will help you to improve you speaking success, then please use the information on the following page or complete and mail the supplied form to me. Throughout the year, I present many seminars and training sessions and I would like to keep you up-to-date about them.

Please note one thing, though: I do *not* take on just anyone as a private client nor do I accept just anyone into my small, exclusive hands-on workshop trainings. I only accept people who are positive, results-oriented people with can-do attitudes. If you are a positive, can-do person that is not afraid to "put the rubber to the road" and *make* your goals and dreams come true, then I look forward to hearing from you.

Probably the most satisfying and gratifying part of what I do is seeing and hearing about the tremendous gains people make in their business using the skills and techniques I teach them. I sincerely hope that you become one of those people.

David R. Portney has been doing trainings, keynote speeches, seminars, and every kind of public speaking you can imagine for over 22 years. He has conducted trainings and talks for major companies such the National Notary Association, The Learning Annex, and The Los Angeles Times.

David's seminars, workshops, books, manuals, and kits instruct you in many ways, including...

- how to completely conquer stage fright and eradicate public speaking fear forever.
- get the behind-the-scenes business side of things so you enjoy profits and not suffer losses.
- get the logistics of organizing your own seminars and prevent chaos and disaster.
- master expert presentation skills practically overnight so you're not fumbling around.
- exactly how to prepare and deliver a stellar presentation every time, even with little or no time to prepare.

Please contact David now to receive information about the products and services he has available that will skyrocket your seminar speaking success!

Address: The American Seminar Academy
PO Box 3555
Redondo Beach, CA 90277-1555

Web: www.SeminarAcademy.com

Email: david@seminaracademy.com

Or complete and mail the handy form on the following page!

Yes! I Would Like More Information About How to Succeed in Seminar & Public Speaking!

Yes, David, please send me information about the products and services you have that will sky-rocket my seminar speaking success and mail it to me at the following address:

Name: _____
_____

Street: _____
_____

City: _____ State/Province:_____

Zip/Postal Code: _____ Country:
_____

Phone: _____

Email:_____

Please check all that apply:

☐ I am or plan to be a professional speaker.

☐ I use or plan to use seminars for my business.

☐ I speak and present seminars for my job.

Please detach this form, affix proper postage, and place in the mail

The American Seminar Academy
c/o David R. Portney
POB 3555
Redondo Beach CA 90277-1555

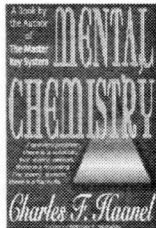

www.SeminarAcademy.com